Advance Praise for *The Art and Science of Staff Fighting*

"*The Art and Science of Staff Fighting* is a treasure trove of knowledge that employs both historic- and traditional-use references along with intriguing theory to convey practical application and very specific, useful, and efficient staff-fighting strategies that are applicable to all martial art styles. Sensei Joe Varady, a world-level weapons fighting competitor with more than thirty years of martial arts experience and a perpetual student of the martial arts in multiple disciplines, shares his vast and seemingly endless knowledge and enlightens readers through a well-described, step-by-step tutorial that draws upon real life-techniques while combining an outstanding pictorial representation of those techniques with active lessons to reinforce what was taught.

"As a longtime staff practitioner, competitor, and instructor, I was overwhelmingly inspired by the personal stories told by this highly accomplished competitor and warrior; the training methodologies shared throughout the text, particularly the home-devised training equipment; and the depth with which the scientific explanations were presented. *The Art and Science of Staff Fighting* is an outstanding reference guidebook that serves the beginner to the most advanced student—there is simply something for everyone and at every level. Sensei Varady has created one of the most practical, interesting, and comprehensive staff-fighting books that I have ever had the pleasure of reading. This will be required reading for all of my weapons students, and this book will be proudly integrated into my personal reference collection."

> —**Michael J. Gallagher**, USA Taekwondo national weapons champion; owner/operator/instructor, Generations Taekwondo; board member, Universal Systems of Martial Arts; 2015 inductee, Philadelphia Historic Martial Arts Society Hall of Fame

"Joe Varady is one of the top weapons experts in our style, known for his in-depth research as well as intense training. He's also a sought-after instructor whose seminars have an enthusiastic following. It's good to see him now sharing some of his knowledge and training methods in this excellent, well-organized book."

> —**Master John Burns**, Cuong Nhu ninth dan; founder and head instructor, Berkeley Cuong Nhu Karate

"Joe Varady not only walks the talk but also is a student of the martial arts, always learning and focused on improving in all aspects of training. He understands details and applications, and puts the action behind every vision in the game called improvement. I was honored to work with him on our style's soft-style manual and know that anything he creates is truly a treasure for anyone's training in the martial arts."

> —**Kirk Farber**, Cuong Nhu Oriental Martial Arts seventh-degree black belt; executive director and founder, Fitness And Character Education (FACE); author, *The Soft Style Training Manual*

"I received a copy of Master Varady's book, *The Art and Science of Staff Fighting*, and dove headfirst into the pages, studying every word. There were three excellent points about this work which distinguish it both as a timeless core resource for all staff training and the principal example of what a martial arts manual should be. These three points are as follows:

"One: A universal application of principles, physics, and physiology. The information Master Varady provides is *truth*. Every word here is true, no matter the style or method. Even though we each may do little things differently, the practice of the various ranges and grips encountered are consistent across the board of styles. Their applications, benefits, and comparability will be the same no matter which school of martial arts you attend. The information here will benefit what you do, while providing you with proper application methods for developing those skills.

"Two: A clear explanation of combative movement. This book does not give you pages of examples of countertechniques and specific applications. Instead, it approaches the combat scenarios and gives you the benefits and shortcomings presented in those situations. This allows the reader to apply the information in all situations, instead of focusing only on learning the movements of the teacher. This is humbling of a master to provide because anyone will directly benefit from this information, without a clear line of lineage or transmission to attribute to Master Varady.

"Three: A total training syllabus. By this, I am referring to the completeness of the program he provides us with. Just as in a university, Professor Varady gives us each a lesson plan (which, of course, is only as fixed as you see fit), with the homework and the study tools."

—**Michael Xia Chongyi**, Daoist swordsman; twenty-sixth-generation
Wudang Dragon Gate Daoist; founder, Wudang Swordsmen Academies,
International; founder, Academia Wudang de México; head referee,
Taiji Fencing League; author, *Sword Dancing Classic*

"When Joe joined my fight school many years ago, I knew there was something special about him. He captured almost every title each year in our tournaments and quickly impressed everyone with his style and speed. If you ever wanted to learn staff fighting but wanted a more 'worldly' approach in place of just Eastern styles, this is the book you have been looking for. Joe Varady is a lifelong martial artist committed to greatness, and this book is a testimonial to his hard work and martial prowess."

—**Dave Dickey**, free scholler, Western martial arts; author, *30 Day Guide to
Creating an Awesome Life*; two-time Martial Arts Hall of Fame nominee;
founder, Live Steel Fight Academy

"In my thirty years of martial arts practice, I have explored quite an array of armed and unarmed systems, and quite a few training manuals. *The Art and Science of Staff Fighting* is that rarest of martial arts publications: a well-written book that presents a fully developed training system with clarity. Sensei Joe Varady has a deep understanding of the dynamics of weapons combat, developed over years of facing actual opponents in real-time contests. As both an educator and a master martial artist, he understands how to build a solid foundation of skills from which the practitioner can develop the flexibility and dynamic flow essential to either artistry or actual combat."

> —**Chris Baglieri**, Instructor, Cuong Nhu Oriental Martial Arts; senior instructor, Kidsafe Youth Programs; certified CPI Nonviolent Crisis Intervention trainer

"This is truly an amazing book that manages to capture Master Joe's passion and love for training and mastering all forms of combat. With equal passion he has distilled and shared that knowledge here. In days of yore, masters would often hoard their experience as a precious commodity and only share their secret 'ancient training techniques' with the most loyal and talented students. Joe has paid the price for every bit of knowledge he has gained in blood, sweat, tears, and unrelenting effort to refine his craft so that he can be a better warrior but also, more importantly, a better teacher."

> —**Shane Forsythe**, Cuong Nhu Oriental Martial Arts first-degree black belt; Haidong Gumdo third-degree black belt

"I met Joe Varady for the first time in Hungary at the WEKAF World Championship. He is an absolutely fair sportsman with a lot of knowledge. We became friends from the first day when we saw each other. It's a big honor for me to know him. In 2015 I got the chance to teach his group, and it felt like family. I would be proud in the future to invite him for a seminar in my dojang. I wish him much success with the book and all the best for life."

> —**Perry Zmugg**, grandmaster, Jung Kwan Jang Nim (hapkido); sifu, wing chun; guro, arnis; author of numerous books and videos including *Skriptum for Real Arnis Level 1–5*; Guinness world record holder; multiple world champion in various events; member of numerous martial art halls of fame

"One of the best bo staff books I have seen. Very informative, well written, easy to follow and understand. Whether you are a beginner or not, this is the book you want to start with!"

> —**Master Paul Cheng**, Cheng's Martial Arts School; author, *Student Manual*

"This book is an excellent guide for martial artists interested in learning the fundamentals of training with a staff and improving their skill set. Each section includes easy-to-follow guidelines and drills for practitioners of all levels of skill and experience. What I found to be most valuable is how each section is broken down into new movement patterns with easy-to-follow guidelines that teach you how to practice the skills in solo training, with a partner, with specially crafted equipment, or as a workout routine. This book also provides insight and instructions for creating training tools for your home or dojo to hone in on your staff skills for solo training and sparring. Joe is an articulate, gifted instructor who excels in breaking down complex movement into easily digestible training modules, and his clarity shines through in this book."

—**Evan Dzierzynski**, Owner/lead coach, NOVA Self Defense

"Expertise shines through this detailed coaching text, which imparts clear instructions, a sense of motivation, and a can-do attitude.

"*The Art and Science of Staff Fighting: A Complete Instructional Guide* by Joe Varady offers all the know-how needed to master this martial art.

"Varady provides history and instruction for every element of staff fighting. As with most of the martial arts, each element of staff fighting—from forms to training processes to combat—has deep history and significance. Varady equips people not only to *do* staff fighting but to *understand* it.

"While external action takes center stage for most of the book, it is always undergirded by the foundation of internal growth and mental focus. This book covers everything from the most basic information ('What is staff fighting?') to involved, technical instruction (fighting multiple opponents). It is organized from simple to complex so that each section logically and practically builds on the last, walking people from their current skill level all the way to mastery. A comprehensive table of contents guides staff fighters of all skill levels to the information they need right now, and sample workouts for each level help take the information off the page and into practice.

"Sensei Joe Varady has been involved in martial arts for decades. His expertise comes through in the detailed nature of the book and in his coaching voice—clear instruction, compelling motivation, and can-do attitude. His energy keeps the momentum of learning moving—a must when training gets tough, as the skills grow in complexity—and his expertise makes sure those who follow his lead are empowered and safe.

"This book is accessible to staff fighters of every skill level, but it's most valuable for beginners in staff fighting who have some experience in other martial arts. Varady's step-by-step instruction, along with their own physical confidence, will jump-start the learning process. Advanced fighters and those who are teaching or coaching others will find this book polishes their skills, gives them tools and language to explain the process, and pushes them to excel at higher levels.

"The book's step-by-step images are helpful, though sometimes a bit small, using arrows to show motion and direction for each posture and motion. The stick figure illustrations, however, don't add much understanding to the text. The stop-motion-like photos that show all parts of a complex action (such as a shoulder roll/somersault while holding the staff) in one photo are impressive as well as helpful.

"*The Art and Science of Staff Fighting* deftly guides potential staff fighters from step one to successful combat."

—**Melissa Wuske**, *Foreword Reviews*

JOE VARADY

The Art and Science of Staff Fighting
A COMPLETE INSTRUCTIONAL GUIDE

YMAA Publication Center
Wolfeboro, NH USA

YMAA Publication Center, Inc.
PO Box 480
Wolfeboro, NH 03894
800 669-8892 • www.ymaa.com • info@ymaa.com

ISBN: 9781594394119 (print) • ISBN: 9781594394126 (ebook)

This book set in Adobe Garamond and Frutiger

Cover design by Axie Breen
Edited by Doran Hunter
Typesetting by Westchester Publishing Services
Illustrations provided by the author

10 9 8 7 6 5 4 3 2

Printed in Canada

Publisher's Cataloging in Publication

Names: Varady, Joe, author.
Title: The art and science of staff fighting / Joe Varady.
Description: Wolfboro, NH USA : YMAA Publication Center, [2016] | Includes bibliographical references
   and index.
Identifiers: ISBN: 978-1-594394-11-9 (print) | 978-1-594394-12-6 (eBook) | LCCN: 2016952098
Subjects: LCSH: Stick fighting—Handbooks, manuals, etc. | Quarter-staff—Handbooks, manuals, etc. |
   Single-stick—Handbooks, manuals, etc. | Staffs (Sticks, canes, etc.)—Handbooks, manuals, etc. | Polearms—
   Handbooks, manuals, etc. | Hand-to-hand fighting—Handbooks, manuals, etc. | BISAC: SPORTS &
   RECREATION / Martial Arts & Self-Defense. | SPORTS & RECREATION / Outdoor Skills.
Classification: LCC: GV1141.2 .V37 2016 | DDC: 796.8—dc23

Acknowledgments

I would like to thank the following people who had a special impact on my staff training over the years (please forgive me if I have overlooked anybody): O Sensei Ngo Dong (founder of Cuong Nhu), Grandmaster Quynh Ngo (head of Cuong Nhu), Sensei Kay Etheridge (my first Eastern bo teacher), Sir Chuck Bennett (knight of the SCA and my first Western quarterstaff teacher), Guro Steve Wolk (Doce Pares Eskrima, six-time world champion), Dr. Mike Rothman (who introduced me to the concept of double striking), Sensei Joe Montague (bokken and jo staff), Sir Dave Dickey (Live Steel Fight Academy, creator of the Three-Step Rule), Swordmaster Joe McGlaughlin (my Live Steel brother), Master Alan Cheung (Shushi no kon dai), Master Mike Ponzio (author of the Cuong Nhu bo manuals), Master John Burns (my monkey bo sifu), Master Didi Goodman, Master Lap Hoang (creator of Van Ly, a Vietnamese two-person staff form), Master Robert First (Cuong Nhu Bo forms 6 and 7), Sensei Mike Arnspiger (Cuong Nhu bo expert), Sensei Michael Oscar (the ultimate uke), Carol Riley (editor extraordinaire), Sensei Madeline Crouse (who helped on so many aspects of this project, from editing to directing), and to Andrea Hilborn (who earned her black belt in Photoshop on this project).

Special Thanks: My wonderful and talented wife, Sensei Kathy Varady, for putting up with all my crazy obsessions; Master Bao Ngo, for his past teachings and continued guidance, both in the martial arts and in life in general, and for providing the foreword to this book; photographer extraordinaire Andrea Hilborn for taking and editing most of the pictures in this book; and to my martial arts brother, Chris Hall, for his exceptional and enlightening appendix to this book, "Fighting Physics: The Mechanics of the Staff."

Models: Joe Varady, Chris Hall, Barry Armour, Aaron McCleod, Thanh Nguyen, Kathy Varady, Dawn White, Madeline Crouse, Michael Oscar, Magnus Sepp, Bryan Feddish, Brian Lesyk, Andy Gajewski, Patricia Cress, Andrea Hilborn, Axel Adalsteinsson, James Lolli, Nick Lolli, Christian Cameron, Sean Hayes, and Quynh Ngo.

Photo Credits: Scooter Girl Photography, Andrea Hilborn, Linda Nikaya, Roland Warzecha, Dawn White, and Ricki Kay.

Table of Contents

Foreword   xiii

Preface   xvii

Introduction   1

   What Is Staff Fighting?   1
   A Brief History of the Staff   2
   Why Art and Science?   4
   Kitchen Kobudo   5
   Know Your Staff   6
   Intensity   7
   The Levels   8

Level 1: The Foundation   9

   Fundamentals   9
   Stances   10
   Basic Striking   11
   Understanding the Lines   13
   Basic Blocking   14
   Evading, Blocking, and Parrying   16
   Footwork   17
   Figure Eights (Downward/Upward)   18
   Level-1 Workout   19

Level 2: Basic Middle Grip   21

   The Fighting Stance   21
   Combat Striking   22
   Range, Distancing, and the Circle of Death   23
   Targeting   25
   Training Equipment: Target Sticks   26
   Combinations   27
   Feinting   31
   Strategy and Tactics   33
   Training Equipment: The Pell   34

Defense: The Wall   38
Level-2 Workout   40

LEVEL 3: Advanced Middle Grip   41
The Double Strike   41
Training Equipment: Target Sticks   42
Hooking Disarms   44
The Push-Pull Energy Drill   48
Training Equipment: The Striking Ball   49
Disarming Blocks   51
Sliding Disarms   53
Shushi's Wall   55
Level-3 Workout   58

LEVEL 4: Basic Extended Grip   59
Introduction to Extended Grip   59
Extended-Grip Basic Strikes   62
Extended-Grip Figure Eights   64
Extended-Grip Thrusting   66
Training Equipment: The Target Ball   67
Training Equipment: The Thrust Board   68
Snap Strikes   69
Training Equipment: The Horizontal Makiwara   70
Extended-Grip Blocking Disarms   71
Level-4 Workout   72

LEVEL 5: Advanced Extended Grip   73
Fencing with the Staff   73
The Change of Engagement   73
The Double Change   75
The Cutover   76
The Beat   77
Extended-Grip Hooking Disarms   78
The Disarm Drill   81
Training Equipment: Spinners   83
Parrying   84
Part the Grass to Find the Snake   87
Level-5 Workout   89

LEVEL 6: Combat with the Staff   91
The Moment of Truth   91
Full-Contact Fighting   92
Training Equipment: The Padded Staff   94
Understanding Timing   95
The Three-Step Rule   96
Programming   97

Continuation of Attack 98
Blitz Attacks 102
Leaping 102
Flèche 103
The Grand Overall Strategy 104
The Seven Principal Rules 106
Level-6 Workout 107

LEVEL 7: Expert Staff Training 109
Hot Stuff 109
Switching Grips 109
Alternate Ready Positions 110
    Fool's Guard 110
    Tail Guard 111
    High Guard 112
    Rear Guard 114
Additional Techniques 118
    Upward Heel Strike 119
    Overhand Heel Thrust 119
    Jabbing Thrusts 121
    Poisonous Snake Coming Out from the Cave 122
    Fiore's Block 123
    Disarming Beat 125
    Trapping and Pinning 126
    Flying Front Kick 127
    Flicking 128
    Throwing 129

LEVEL 8: Master Staff Training 131
Close Combat with the Staff 131
Groundwork 136
Facing Multiple Opponents with the Staff 141
Unarmed Defense against the Staff 149

LEVEL 9: The Way of the Spear 159
Intro to the Spear 159
Basic Spear Fighting Strategy 160
Training Equipment: The Rings 162
Unarmed Defense against a Spear 163
Throwing the Spear 166
Catching the Spear 168
Tub Tilting 170

Appendix I: Fighting Physics: The Mechanics of the Staff 173
The Big Three 173
Striking 175

Kinetic Energy   175
Dynamics   176
Angle of Impact   176
Striking Surface: Smaller Is Better   177
Blocking and Parrying   178
The Wall   179
The Wet Blanket (and Subsequent Counterattack)   181
Parrying   181
Levers   182
Uprooting Lever (Second-Class Lever)   183
Pushing Lever (Third-Class Lever)   185
The Kinetic Chain   186
Conclusions   187
About Chris Hall   188

Appendix II: Additional Skills and Drills   189
Recommended Reading   201
About the Author   203

Foreword

Whether you are looking to amp up your staff-fighting game or learning for the first time, this book is for you. Joe Varady is one of the top stick fighters in the world, both in short sticks and in staff fighting. In 2014 I had the opportunity to help coach him in preparation for the World Eskrima Kali Arnis Federation's world championships in Hungary. After months of at times torturous training, Joe came back victorious, having placed fourth in the world in men's heavyweight full-contact double short-stick fighting, and second in the world in men's light heavyweight full-contact staff fighting.

In this book he brings together over three decades of training experience to create a generous, logical, step-by-step program to enable you to train as well.

As a staff fighter, Joe isn't just fast and powerful; he is a master of the weapon itself, and of strategy. He is proficient in using all parts of the staff in many different ways, and he constantly hones his ability to anticipate an opponent's movements, take effective countermeasures, and transition smoothly to avoid being hit.

Joe's core martial art style is Cuong Nhu, which was founded in 1965 in the old capital of Hue, Vietnam, by my father, Grandmaster Ngo Dong. Cuong Nhu (Vietnamese for "hard" and "soft") has its roots in Shotokan karate, combined with principles drawn from aikido, judo, wing chun, Vovinam, taijiquan, and boxing. Cuong Nhu practitioners train with many weapons, but our foundational weapons training is in short stick, long staff, and spear. These are the weapons that have historically—and in many cultures—been most easily accessible to ordinary people for self-defense.

Cuong Nhu is a style that focuses on self-improvement, community service, and love and respect for others. We strive to be more than just another form of martial art. We ask our practitioners to apply the skills and discipline they learn through training toward becoming better people and helping others less fortunate. This has been true since Cuong Nhu's earliest days in war-torn Vietnam, through the founding of the first US schools at the University of Florida in Gainesville (when my father came to the US in 1971 to pursue his doctorate), and through to the present day.

Joe Varady has always stood out for his passion, dedication, and leadership skills. His outsize personality and entertaining approach to teaching and learning make training fun for his students—kids and adults alike. They even make things fun for his teachers. He is respectful but constantly inquisitive. His desire to be a better martial artist is never ending, and his thirst for knowledge extends beyond the physical and practical to the historical and cultural as well. He constantly seeks ways to give back—to his students, his community, and the style. And his enthusiasm for fighting with weapons is undeniable, especially with the staff.

You've heard the old saying, "Nothing great was ever achieved without enthusiasm." Joe lives by it. I still remember the first time I visited his dojo outside Philadelphia for a special seminar and rank testing. I had heard stories about his amazing "home dojo" and

The Varady home dojo.

Joe and Bao.

the various exploits that allegedly took place there. I was pleased to be invited to stay at his home, and I looked forward to getting a tour. He showed me around with great enthusiasm, and it was impressive. There behind his house, he had built a traditional Asian-style dojo worthy of a Bruce Lee movie. There was a main training floor framed by various weapons racks and several smaller partitioned areas dedicated to specialties such as knife throwing, wing chun–dummy training, and grappling.

His weapons collection went beyond the usual staples of Far East Asian arts to include European weapons such as broadswords and shields, spiked balls and chains, fencing foils, and chain mail. What an impressive array of weapons to practice and play with, conveniently located right behind the house! Over the course of the long weekend, when we weren't busy with the seminar and testing at the main dojo, the senior instructors, Joe, and I would spar each other using different weapons in a variety of formats: one on one, one versus many, or what we called "war mode," where two sides with various weapons would line up across the dojo floor and clash with one another. Depending on the types of weapons and whether or not they were padded, we would don appropriate protective gear or armor and go at it. A measure of realism, with actual contact and the need to attack, defend, move, and react in an instant, all combined to make the training intensely fun and effective.

Now, with this book, you too can get a look inside Joe's home dojo, take some private lessons, and get started on the path toward mastery of fighting with the staff.

Master Bao Ngo

Tenth-degree black belt

Cuong Nhu Oriental Martial Arts

Nashville, Tennessee

Preface

When I was about twelve years old, I discovered the martial arts watching kung fu movies on TV. Saturday afternoons were more than entertainment for me; they were pure inspiration. In a short time I was twirling an old broomstick in the backyard, and so began my lifelong love of the martial arts. That was over thirty years ago. Today, my primary passion (apart from raising my two wonderful kids, Cosmos and Kayla) is to train and teach the martial arts, especially when it comes to the staff.

Over the past three decades, I have trained in Eastern martial arts such as karate, gongfu, taekwondo, judo, jujitsu, wing chun, and eskrima (to name a few), along with various Western martial arts, including boxing, fencing, long sword, sword and shield, and several methods of armored fighting. I wrote six training manuals for my core style, Cuong Nhu Oriental Martial Arts, and worked on another for my main Western martial arts school, Live Steel Fight Academy.

I had the privilege of learning from many dedicated and knowledgeable instructors and have had numerous sparring partners over the years. I owe each of them a debt of gratitude for their part, large or small, in adding to my martial knowledge. Combine these many experiences with my love for researching and writing about martial arts training, and the result is the book you are now reading.

In this book, I provide a logical progression of combat training with the staff. It is an interstylistic, multicultural approach that you can easily incorporate into any martial art. Take from it what you can and save the rest for later. Constantly keep seeking new information, both from outside sources and, perhaps more importantly, from within. Keep an open mind, practice, explore, and add to your knowledge and skills whenever you can. If you study hard, then train even harder. The result will be your own personal fighting method with the staff, based upon sound principles and techniques.

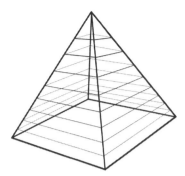

Introduction

What Is Staff Fighting?

The staff has been a common weapon worldwide since ancient times. Over the ages, humans have used this basic weapon for self-defense and for contest. Fighting with the quarterstaff was once so popular that it was included in the *Boy Scout Handbook,* but it has since fallen out of fashion among combat martial arts. While the *eskrimadors* of the Philippines have done much in the last several decades to promote combat arts with the short stick worldwide, little has been done to preserve and progress the art of fighting with the long stick or staff.

Today, top practitioners of the staff are often veterans of the karate tournament circuit, performing incredible twirls with foil-covered balsa wood staves, throwing in flips and full splits for dramatic effect. While I appreciate these practitioners for their tremendous physical prowess and dazzling artistry, these performances are more art than martial.

Tracing these contemporary staff forms back in time, we find their roots in much less extravagant, more traditional, Asian staff forms. In fact, Eastern forms evolved originally from prearranged drills undoubtedly performed with a partner. When no partner was available, it was beneficial to practice the moves alone. Eventually, various combinations of techniques were linked together, creating longer forms, or kata. Somewhere along the line (in Asia, at least), the partner work seems to have become lost in favor of the solo performance, the vestiges practiced as secondary *bunkai* or applications. These were eventually stylized into prearranged practice sets that usually lack the realism of actual combat.

The Western martial arts, however, never developed long solo forms, concentrating instead on combat drills and free fighting. This is not to say that Eastern forms are without merit. Quite the contrary, I have found that, like the yin and yang, training in one complements training in the other.

In this book, I present the best of the Eastern and Western traditions (along with a few in between), unified seamlessly to create a modern, logical, progressive, compact, and culturally diverse system of staff fighting that is easy to learn and applicable to any practitioner from any style.

I have learned many staff forms over the years, and some I still practice to this day. While it would be incorrect to say that forms have no value in training for combat, forms, whether performed solo or with a partner, are usually very difficult to apply in a free fighting format, and yet they claim to teach effective fighting methods. I have found, through experience, that if you want to learn to fight with the staff, it is best to focus on staff fighting itself, not on a rote mimicry of fighting.

A Brief History of the Staff

The long stick, commonly known as a staff, is certainly one of the oldest and most universal weapons in human history. In prehistory, before metal or even stone spear points were attached to the ends of sticks, the staff was used for self-defense. They were made of hardwood and of a length that usually depended on their intended use. For example, shorter staves were used for walking sticks, while some, nine feet or more in length, were used to pole riverboats. Due to its similarity to hoes, spades, or other long-handled tools, the staff was often a practical weapon in agricultural communities where the peasant or common man was unable to purchase swords or other metal weapons. It should be no surprise that staff-fighting systems originated in many countries around the world. Today, staff techniques can still be performed with common household items, such as brooms or garden tools.

In the Asian martial arts, the staff is often considered the "king of weapons" for its ability to exploit the weaknesses of other weapons. The oldest recorded staff-fighting techniques can be found in China, where systemized *gùn* (rod or stick) techniques are thousands of years old. Chinese staffs are commonly made of white wax wood, while bamboo staffs, called *lathi,* were used in India. In the Philippines, the rattan staff, called a *sibat,* is common, while in Vietnam the staff is known as *truong con* and is usually made of rattan-like "spear bamboo." In Okinawa, the staff is called *kon,* and is traditionally made from red or white oak. In Japan, *bojitsu* was organized about 1300 A.D., and it is from this art that we get the popular term *bo* (staff), the full name of which is *rokushakubo* ("six foot staff").

In Europe, where it was often called the "quarterstaff," recorded fighting methods date back to fifteenth-century manuals from Germany. Popularized in the sixteenth-century English ballads and tales of Robin Hood, European authors seem to agree that the quarterstaff was among the best, if not the very best, of all handheld weapons.

Today, the most common staff length is about equal to the user's height. This is a versatile length, long enough for good reach but short enough to allow quicker manipulation than a longer staff. It should, however, be remembered that each variant has its own advantages and disadvantages. A longer staff has an obvious reach advantage, while a shorter staff usually has

Staff manuals have been around for a very long time. An illustration from an anonymous German codex written in 1591.

less weight and thus a speed advantage. At approximately one inch in diameter, a staff can be of uniform diameter throughout its entire length or taper in width from the center outward to either end. Some staves even have noncircular cross sections, such as hexagons or octagons, that allow the striking power to be focused onto an edge, dramatically increasing the pounds of pressure per square inch that can be delivered into the target (more about that later).

Note that it is the quality of your martial training that is of paramount importance, not the specifications of your weapon. If you are ever forced to defend yourself or your loved ones, the odds are that you will not have your regular weapons with you. Instead, you will have to improvise and effectively wield whatever weapon may be at hand, be it long or short, light or heavy, sharp or blunt. Therefore, we must attempt to improve our odds by training with a variety of weapons at a variety of ranges.

This is why the legendary samurai Miyamoto Musashi stressed in his famous work *The Book of Five Rings* that you should not favor any particular weapon.

That said . . .

I love the staff!

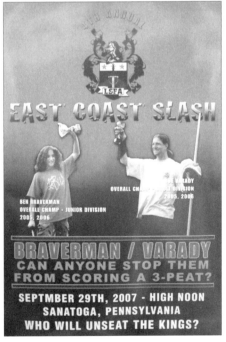

Live Steel Fight Academy's 2007 tournament poster.

Why Art and Science?

The title of this book, *The Art and Science of Staff Fighting*, speaks to the dual nature of combat. Art and science, like the yin and yang, are two halves of a larger whole. On one hand, you have art, which finds its roots in human instinct and displays itself through self-expression. Science, on the other hand, draws from empirical observation, analysis of data, and the identification of patterns. Each of these, both art and science, plays a crucial role in your success in combat.

For centuries traditional Asian martial artists in particular have used their martial studies as vehicles for personal exploration and spiritual growth. Dedicated training develops self-confidence, self-control, and physical coordination. The practitioners' goal is *mushin*, a state of non-thinking, or "no-mind." They are urged to look past the overt physical movements of the techniques to find a deeper, more meaningful purpose to their practice, that of achieving, if only for a moment, a supreme state of mind described as *satori:* a moment of self-realization, of complete understanding.

While this is all well and good, any reliable system of self-defense needs to be rooted in science. Understanding the physical and psychological principles underpinning the combat you are engaging in can put you at a decided advantage over your opponent. Physically, it is important to understand the nature of the weapon, in this

case the staff, and how it may be used to greatest effect. How you stand, generate power, and even what part of the staff you strike with all have a tremendous impact on the success or failure of your technique. Psychologically, you need to understand how your opponents think and how to manipulate their responses and behaviors through processes such as "programming."

In the end, art and science fuse into one, and the results reflect the level of the practitioner. Train hard. Study hard. Grow. Succeed.

Perceive that which cannot be seen.
—Miyamoto Musashi

Kitchen Kobudo

My instructor looked more like a janitor than a karate teacher when he arrived for the day's seminar. Before us he laid out a telephone (they had cords back in those days!), a telephone book (I am really starting to date myself, aren't I?), a bucket, some rags, a bottle of spray cleaner (actually just water), a scrub brush, a dustpan, and a broom. He told us each to select an item, find a partner, and take our places on the floor. We spent the next few hours exploring how we would go about fighting with our new "weapons." He called the session "Kitchen Kobudo."

Kobudo is a term used to describe the traditional weapons systems of Okinawa. It is often taught (perhaps erroneously) that their principal weapons—such as the tonfa, nunchaku, and sai—evolved from farm implements and other everyday items. Chief among these was the *rokushakubo*, or six-foot staff, commonly referred to as a "bo." It could have developed from a tool called a *tenbin*: a carrying-stick placed across the shoulders with baskets or sacks hanging from either end.

The sad fact is that you will probably not have a staff handy when you need it most. Luckily, our environment is usually full of improvised weapons; you just need to learn how to recognize them. Just about any rigid object over three feet long can be used as a makeshift staff. Staff-fighting techniques can be effectively applied in a self-defense situation using a variety of everyday objects, such as a walking stick, coatrack, curtain rod, floor lamp, hockey stick, fallen tree branch, broom, mop, shovel, or rake.

The staff has one important advantage over most other weapons, and that is its superior reach. Being able to strike or otherwise engage opponents without their being able to strike you back puts you at a distinct advantage, one that is especially important if your attacker happens to be armed with an edged weapon. Therefore, studying staff-fighting techniques should be an important part of any well-rounded martial curriculum.

Know Your Staff

1. Practice until the staff becomes a natural extension of your body.

2. Even in practice, strive to strike sharply and block solidly at all times.

3. Heavier staves hit harder and are better for blocking. However, their mass makes them slower. Heavy staves are good for developing the muscles used in manipulating the staff.

4. Lighter staves are faster, generally don't hit as hard, and can break when put under the stress of a hard strike or block. Lighter weapons are usually preferred for forms and free fighting.

5. A shiny protective finish can hinder sliding smoothly from one grip to another, so if your hand squeaks as you slide it along the staff, you should sand it.

6. Carefully inspect your weapon before each workout by running your hands gently along its length, feeling for any splinters. They will need to be sanded off or taped over before use.

7. Personalize your fighting style, working to integrate your staff skills with your chosen foundation art or primary method of self-defense.

8. Realize that learning any new skill takes time. Learn gradually and take the time to master each level before moving on to the next.

The man who moves a mountain must start by moving small stones.
—Chinese proverb

Intensity

The most distinguishing factor in any effective performance, be it in forms or fighting, is intensity.

Without intensity, a martial artist appears disconnected from his work, and any martial endeavor that he attempts to undertake will lack an essential ingredient.

So what exactly makes a performance "intense"? It begins with the eyes. Cultivate a look of determination, intention, and absolute seriousness. It should permeate your entire body. Focus your mind, concentrating every fiber of your being on the task at hand.

You should not be overly tense, as tension will slow your reaction time. Seek a state of ready relaxation, clear your mind of doubt, and fill yourself with the confidence to succeed.

I call this shift "flipping the switch" because that is how it feels to me. One moment I can be lighthearted and laughing, but when it comes time to perform, my whole demeanor changes. My intent focuses. I feel it most in my eyes; it is where I begin to dominate my opponent, as though I were going to overcome him solely with my will.

When the mind is completely focused, the intensity shows physically through the body in your performance. Moves become quicker and stronger, with more focus, reflecting your intent. Without spirit and intensity, the martial arts are reduced to mere movements with little meaning or practical, effective application.

There are added benefits to developing this intensity. It can be applied to all aspects of your life. Learn to live as intensely as you practice, increasing the quality of your life experience and enriching the lives and experiences of others. It's this quality that makes the martial arts a unique vehicle for personal growth and continued evolution.

The Levels

My staff system is divided into logical stages of training, both for ease of learning and for developing an understanding of the underpinnings of staff combat. The first five levels include workouts specifically designed to help you master the basic material.

Level 1: The Foundation. These are the basics upon which we will build a complete fighting style. This level begins with nine basic strikes, basic applications, and a twirl. The aim is to get you comfortable with properly swinging a staff, as well as learning to safely make contact with a partner's staff. This is the level at which most traditional staff training ends, but for us it is only the beginning!

Level 2: Basic Middle Grip. Topics covered include combat striking, targeting, developing combinations, feinting, as well as some important blocking concepts. It is not enough just to read the information. Build the training equipment, complete the workouts, and watch your skills improve.

Level 3: Advanced Middle Grip. Here you'll encounter sophisticated, "3-D" concepts on how to use the staff: advanced middle-grip double striking and hooking disarms.

Level 4: Basic Extended Grip. This level involves long-range fighting using the extended grip. It is almost like learning a whole new weapon. Combined with your knowledge of middle-grip fighting, your newfound range will keep your attackers at bay.

Level 5: Advanced Extended Grip. We start with techniques inspired by Western fencing. Add to this some very effective entry methods, and you will have all the skills necessary to become a formidable fighter at both middle and long range.

Level 6: Combat with the Staff. Time to suit up and start fighting! Included are guidelines for full-contact training, plans for constructing your own padded weapons, and tips on fighting. The highlight, however, is my secret formula to success: The Grand Overall Strategy. Get ready to *rock!*

Level 7: Expert Training. Imagine a trip to the salad bar. Level 1 is the bowl, providing the basic structure. Levels 2–4 make up the lettuce in our salad, while level 5 is the fork that allows us to eat (level 6). But what is a salad without toppings? Boring, that's what! Level 7 is your complete toppings bar, full of lots of additional techniques to spice up your staff-fighting salad.

Level 8: Master Training. Advanced staff-fighting concepts include close combat, unarmed defense against the staff, and facing multiple opponents. You will need all the skills you learned in levels 1–7 to be successful.

Level 9: The Way of the Spear. As if your staff-fighting skills were not effective enough, add a sharp blade to the end, and you are really cooking with gas. (Warning: Spear training is dangerous and *not* for beginners!)

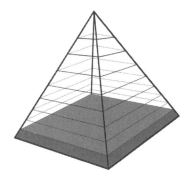

The Foundation

Fundamentals

Staff fighting begins with learning a system of basic strikes and blocks. Training at this level is about familiarizing yourself with the staff, learning how to hold and wield it correctly. We are not concerned with combat application . . . yet. The nine basic strikes provide a foundation and framework upon which we can then build a system of practical fighting techniques. To accomplish this, we are going to borrow the Oriental concept of *kata*.

A kata is a sequence—also known as a "form"—of prearranged moves performed solo against an invisible opponent. This basic kata is made up of only nine simple moves. Since we are primarily concerned with combat, we will not be using a formal salute or bow; however, if your style uses one and you wish to incorporate it, feel free to do so.

When performing the basics, stand in a ready stance. Hold the staff in a standard middle grip, with your left hand palm down and your right hand palm up. Your hands are about one shoulder width apart, dividing the staff into equal thirds. This puts your right hand in the dominant position (if you are left handed, feel free to reverse everything). The right end of the staff is called the tip, and is marked with white in the photos, while the left end, or heel, is marked with black.

There are nine basic strikes, divided into four types: downward, upward, horizontal, and thrusts. Each strike starts from its own chamber or load-up, which is a ready position for each technique, not unlike drawing your fist back before punching. Then both arms are used in a pushing-pulling motion to accelerate the staff through the target. For ease of training, diagonal strikes are initially delivered on a 45-degree angle. In the finished position, your front arm is straight but not locked. Assume your target is directly in front of you. The staff strikes through the target, then stops abruptly on a 45-degree angle past the target, using your whole body as a brake to rapidly stop the staff. Since the staff is striking your upper arms, in the beginning the percussion may result in some bruising. These bruises, which we refer to as "bo bruises," rarely return with the same intensity, and are often worn as temporary badges of honor by beginners who bear them proudly as a reflection of hard work and dedication to training.

Level-1 basic strikes should be included as a warm-up exercise for any staff training session. Reaching with the weapon will stretch the same muscles in your arms and back that you will be using during your workout. Start slowly, gradually increasing your speed and intensity, all the while keeping perfect form.

Stances

Stances are ways to stand that allow you to fight with the staff effectively. There are three basic stances you will need to be familiar with: the ready stance, the forward stance, and the back stance. The ready stance is a good neutral position and the one most commonly used when holding the staff in middle grip, while forward and back stances are predominately used when you are holding the staff in extended grip.

Ready Stance: In the ready stance, you stand with your feet about shoulder width apart, one foot slightly ahead of the other, with your weight distributed evenly between both feet. This stance offers you quick movements in all directions.

Ready stance

Forward Stance: To assume a forward stance, start from a ready stance and slide your front foot forward until your stance is about twice your shoulder width, from front to back. Bend your front knee, shifting your weight slightly forward so that two-thirds rest on the front foot and one-third on the rear. The forward stance gives you more range and puts more power into your strikes.

Back Stance: To assume a back stance, shift your weight backward so that two-thirds rest on the back foot and only one-third rests on the front. It is common for right-handed fighters to lead with their left foot in the back stance. Stay low, coiled like a snake ready to strike. Always keep both knees flexed, because a straight front leg can easily be broken by a strong kick or strike to the knee. The

Forward stance

Back stance

back stance is used to hover just out of range of your opponent until you see an opportunity to strike.

Basic Striking

In this book, I will refer to the first strike as a "number-1 strike," the second as a "number-2 strike," and so on.

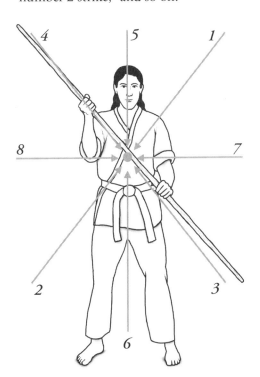

1. Diagonally downward from right to left

2. Diagonally upward from left to right

3. Diagonally upward from right to left

4. Diagonally downward from left to right

5. Vertically downward through the centerline with the tip

6. Vertically upward through the centerline with the heel

7. Horizontally from right to left

8. Horizontally from left to right

9. Thrust to the center with the heel of the staff

Understanding the Lines

To become an effective staff fighter, there are a great many concepts with which you will need to become familiar. Two important concepts that you need to understand are the line of attack and the centerline.

Line of Attack: The line of attack is any path you could take to strike the opponent. The high line encompasses the head and upper body, the midline generally describes the midsection and lower abdomen, while the low line generally refers to the groin, legs, and feet. If an opponent's staff blocks a particular path, then that line is *closed*. If there are no obstructions between you and the target, then that line of attack is *open*. A good staff fighter knows not only how to open a closed line on the opponent, but also how to close any open lines of attack on him- or herself.

Centerline: The concept of the centerline is common to many martial arts, including Western boxing and wing chun gongfu. When you stand square to an opponent, your centerline runs bilaterally down the center of your body, from nose to navel. Many of your most vulnerable target areas lie on this line, including the nose, throat, solar plexus, and groin. You therefore want to protect your centerline from attack.

Offensively, if you can align your centerline with your line of attack, you can bring both ends of your staff to bear on the target. If you were to turn your body sideways to the opponent, you can only strike effectively with one side of your body or one end of the staff. You can use footwork to keep the opponent on your centerline, while staying off the opponent's centerline yourself, making it more difficult for him to strike you.

Basic Blocking

Once you've mastered the basic strikes, you are ready to perform them with a partner, one playing the role of the attacker and the other the defender. While the attacker is

practicing the specific strikes, the defender is learning how to block them.

At this stage, the first four blocks look just like the diagonal strikes they are intended to block, with the focal point midway between the two partners. This is acceptable blocking at this stage of training because it is a relatively safe way of introducing you to making contact with the opponent's weapon. Later, these same blocks will be used to effectively attack the hands (level 3: disarming blocks).

Block of a number-1 strike: downward diagonal, right to left.

Block of a number-2 strike: upward diagonal, left to right.

Block of a number-3 strike: upward diagonal, right to left.

Block of a number-4 strike: downward diagonal, left to right.

Block of a number-5 strike: downward vertical.

Block of a number-6 strike: upward vertical.

Block of a number-7 strike: horizontal, right to left.

Block of a number-8 strike: horizontal, left to right.

Block of a number-9 strike: parry of a thrust to the center.

Moves 5 through 8 are wall blocks, which we will look at in more detail in level 2. Block number 9 isn't really a block at all, but a parry, which is explained in the next section.

Evading, Blocking, and Parrying

There are three basic ways of defending against an incoming attack: you can choose to block, parry, or evade. Your decision will often be dictated by the circumstances of the situation; however, understanding the differences between them is the first step to employing these different strategies effectively. Knowledge and practice leads to understanding.

Evasion consists of ducking, jumping, or using footwork to move you out of the path of the attack. The simplest form of evasion is to move backward out of range of the attack, which usually also puts you out of range to counterattack. More sophisticated evasion techniques can remove you from the path of the weapon while placing you in a good position from which to launch a counterattack. However, these are considered advanced skills that rely on being able to read your opponent's intentions and respond appropriately.

The difference between blocking and parrying is the difference between stopping and sliding. Blocking implies that you bring the opponent's weapon to a standstill, usually by meeting it with an equal but opposite force, while parrying means you redirect the course of your opponent's weapon while still allowing it to remain in motion. It takes considerably more force to block, bringing an opponent's weapon to rest, than it does to parry, causing it to shift course from its intended target.

To block effectively you need to stop the opponent's staff. The mechanics of doing so quickly and efficiently are pretty precise: you either have to meet that incoming force head on with equal force, or you have to act as a kinetic energy absorber, bringing the opponent's weapon to a standstill by sapping it of its momentum. This is discussed in detail later in appendix I, "Fighting Physics: The Mechanics of the Staff," by Chris Hall, which appears at the end of this book.

The ninth block of the basic striking and blocking set is a parry. As the opponent attacks, intercept his thrusting strike with a perpendicular staff moved on a trajectory nearly parallel to that of the incoming weapon, redirecting it slightly but safely off its intended line of attack.

When executed softly, with dexterity and good timing, your block should be almost imperceptible. The opponent should hardly register that you have intercepted his attack until he has overcommitted to his thrust, leaving him momentarily open to a speedy counterattack.

Footwork

Footwork is essential to hitting your opponent without getting hit yourself, which is really the whole point of staff fighting. The general rule on footwork is to keep your body weight balanced over a stable but fluidly mobile base, staying light on the balls of your feet at all times.

Shuffling: Basic footwork with the staff comes in two types: the shuffle and the step. Shuffling is performed much like boxing footwork, with your lead foot taking a small step in the direction you want to go, quickly followed by the trailing foot. To move forward, move your front foot, followed by your rear foot. To move backward, take a small step back with your rear foot, followed by your front. In the same way, step with your left foot to move left and your right foot to move right.

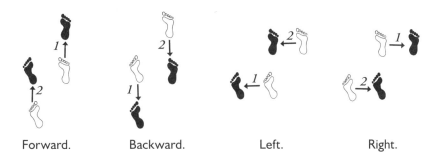

Forward.   Backward.   Left.   Right.

Stepping: You can also do a full step forward or backward, which not only covers more ground, but allows you to switch your stance. Miyamoto Musashi states in his classic treatise *The Book of Five Rings* that the most devastating strikes are performed with this type of footwork. Although he was speaking mainly of the sword, the same holds true for the staff, because the stepping motion puts more of your mass and momentum into the strike. Although there are footwork patterns that step left and right, I do not recommended them because they involve crossing the feet, which puts you in a vulnerable position, albeit momentarily.

Stepping forward.   Stepping backward.

Figure Eights (Downward/Upward)

While at first twirling may seem like just a flashy exercise, spinning the staff around like a cheerleader with a giant baton, becoming familiar with and learning how to manipulate the staff is an important part of combat training. A quick twirl, called a *flurry*, can confuse an opponent while disguising your intentions, setting you up for unexpected angles of attack. You can use a figure eight to parry an opponent's weapon before quickly striking with the other end. Defensively, you can use a twirl to escape from a tie-up or evade a disarm attempt.

The simple downward figure eight consists of four consecutive strikes with the staff. Begin from a standard ready position, with your right hand palm up and your left hand palm down, holding the staff diagonally from your left hip to your right shoulder. Drop the tip of your staff back and to the right (1). Bring your left arm across your body (2) and begin sweeping the tip up and forward (3) into a right-to-left downward diagonal strike with the tip of the staff (4), immediately followed by another right-to-left downward diagonal strike using the heel (5). These strikes are followed by a left-to-right downward diagonal strike with the tip (6), followed by a left-to-right downward diagonal strike with the heel (back to 1). Repeat the motions, practicing them until you can perform all the strikes smoothly and flow them seamlessly into one fluid motion.

Upward figure eights can be a little more difficult at first, but with practice they can be just as smooth and fast as your downward figure eights. When first learning this twirl, begin doing downward figure eights, then slow and finally stop your motion. Reverse the direction of your staff, backtracking along the same path, only now in an upward direction, alternating striking diagonally upward from left to right and from right to left.

As you move your hands closer together, you can twirl faster, but your strikes will lack the leverage and therefore the power of a wider grip.

Level-1 Workout

Objective: To work the basic strikes with the staff, both solo and with a partner, until you have developed sufficient muscle memory that they become fluid and natural. This means working past the point of fatigue so that your body is forced to find the most efficient method to perform each technique. To that end, the same strikes are repeated again and again, but with the different footwork patterns that must also be mastered. You must work until your body and weapon become one.

Warm-Up: Five to ten minutes of downward figure eights, first slowly and gradually getting faster, followed by upward figure eights, both stationary and moving.

Basic Strikes: Perform the following drills one to three times each. First, do each one solo, striking the air and concentrating on using proper body mechanics. Then practice them all again with a partner. Alternate striking and blocking.

1. Perform the nine basic strikes stationary, leading with your right leg.
2. Perform the nine basic strikes stationary, leading with your left leg.
3. Perform the nine basic strikes, advancing with a shuffle on every strike.
4. Perform the nine basic strikes, retreating with a shuffle on every strike.
5. Perform the nine basic strikes, advancing and retreating with the shuffle. Move forward on the first strike and back on the next. Then perform two moves forward followed by two moves back. Then do three moves.
6. Perform the nine basic strikes, advancing with a step on every strike.
7. Perform the nine basic strikes, retreating with a step on every strike.
8. Perform the nine basic strikes, alternating advancing and retreating with each step. Step forward on the first strike and back on the second. Next, perform two steps forward followed by two moves back. Then repeat the pattern with three steps forward followed by three steps back.
9. Perform the nine basic strikes using a circling footwork, stepping left.
10. Perform the nine basic strikes using a circling footwork, stepping right.
11. Complete this workout several times a week for a few weeks, both solo and with a partner. At first you may find this repetitious and boring. But by sticking with it you will prove your commitment and personal discipline to yourself. Training seriously and being consistent will increase your skills with the staff dramatically.

I recommend keeping a training log to record each time you work out with the staff, including a short synopsis of the material you covered in each workout. Set a goal for yourself, such as training a minimum number of days or hours each week or performing the above workout a set number of times (I suggest at least ten times). Setting attainable short-term goals is a good way to stay motivated and achieve your larger goal of becoming technically proficient at staff fighting.

Training Log/Notes:

Sample Entry

11/5 Sat. 60 min. Did the level-1 workout. I now know the nine basic strikes, but stepping while doing them is still a challenge. I think I may have been too tense because my shoulders are sore. Goal for next time: better footwork and relax!

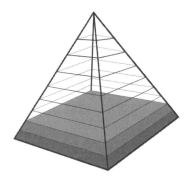

LEVEL 2
Basic Middle Grip

Level 2 is very similar to level 1 because the moves stay the same; however, now that you have a handle on the basics, we can begin to focus on combat application over basic skill acquisition.

The Fighting Stance

In level 2, we introduce the fighting stance or combat stance. From a defensive standpoint, this stance helps protect your most vulnerable target areas. Offensively, you are lighter on your feet and coiled for shorter, faster striking.

To assume a combat stance, start by bending your knees slightly and subtly shifting your weight forward onto the balls of your feet. Adopting the combat stance lowers your center of gravity, allowing you to drop your weight and root yourself, as if bracing against an incoming attack. Hollow out your stomach and roll your shoulders forward. Tuck your chin slightly. This puts you into a protective half-crouch ready position similar to that used by boxers. Also, as in boxing, pivot on the balls of your feet to get your hips into your strikes. At the same time, try to keep your toes pointed toward the opponent as much as possible to keep your body facing him.

Level 1   *Level 2*

The staff is held in middle grip, as described in level 1. This creates a middle section for blocking and more leverage for stronger striking than a closer grip. In middle grip, the advantage lies in wielding a double-ended weapon, dividing the opponent's attention. By keeping both ends equally forward, you keep your opponent guessing which end will strike next.

A variation is to point the tip of your staff at the opponent's throat. This takes away your ability to execute a full strike with the tip, but allows you to thrust the tip at the attacker. Snap striking, which we will cover at level 5, provides a method of striking that can still be delivered effectively with the tip from this guard.

Combat Striking

At level 2, the diagonal strikes are often delivered on a slightly steeper 70-degree angle, striking from shoulder to hip. This makes them considerably more difficult to duck or evade than the 45-degree strikes used in level 1. In the next section, on targeting, you will see how a diagonal strike is capable of hitting on any angle in that quadrant.

Ducking: A number-1 strike delivered on a 45-degree angle (picture 1) is more easily evaded than a steeper 70-degree strike to the same target (picture 2).

When thinking of combat applications, speed is of the essence in successfully striking your opponent. Unlike the full chamber motions used to load up for each strike in level 1, your strikes should become somewhat more compact, with shorter load-ups, but retain all the power of a full strike. This can be a little tricky at first as it requires a subtle but sharp snapping of the hips into your technique. Odd-numbered basic strikes—those that hit with the tip and generally move from right to left—can benefit from an internal rotation toward your body, using your wrists and hands at the moment of contact (the same wringing motion that is used in kendo to add focus to a sword strike). The opposing forces steady the weapon and drive it through the target. However, the mechanics of the offside, even-numbered strikes—those that strike with the heel of the staff—do not lend themselves to the wringing motion. Instead, they rely mostly on a push-pull of the arms, pushing forward with your lead hand while pulling back with your rear, combined with a sharp hip twist for maximum power.

Basic Sources of Power for the Staff

Torque your hands inward.   The push-pull of the arms.   Push, pull, and twist the hip.

Range, Distancing, and the Circle of Death

You must develop a tacit understanding of different ranges and how to properly distance yourself with (or without) the staff in your hands. Proper distancing usually means positioning yourself just outside your opponent's striking range.

The shortest range with the staff is the heel strike. Strikes with the heel of the staff are therefore usually reserved for close-quarters combat. Strikes with the tip have the next greatest range, and it is just outside of this range that you will usually want to position yourself when not striking. It keeps you relatively safe while you look for the proper opportunity to initiate an attack.

To hit anything at a greater range, the opponent will have to move his feet. By keeping your eyes on your opponent's body, you will, with training, be able to see any foot

movements. This should give you ample opportunity to step back yourself, maintaining the distance between you and the opponent, keeping you outside the effective striking range of his staff. Footwork and distancing are interrelated skills that you must develop fully to fight effectively with the staff. A skillful staff fighter controls the fight by controlling the distance, which is accomplished by reading the opponent's movements and then applying the appropriate footwork.

Some examples of range: The maximum range of an average middle grip strike with the tip of the staff (top left), does not come close to the range of an extended grip sliding thrust (top right), while getting any decent amount of range with a heel strike usually requires making a complete step forward with your rear foot (left).

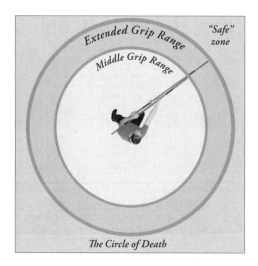

The Circle of Death

It is helpful if you can visualize the "circle of death," the imaginary line around you describing your effective range with the staff. Minimal energy should be expended on any opponent who remains outside this circle; however, whenever an opponent enters your circle, he should be attacked immediately and without hesitation.

You don't always have to wait for your opponent to enter your circle. You can move your circle of death forward by stepping toward the opponent.

Your circle is slightly smaller when you hold the staff in middle grip than when you are using extended grip, but this does not mean that extended grip is superior. Both grips have their own set of advantages and disadvantages. Extended grip is introduced at level 4.

Targeting

As opposed to bladed weapons that slice or stab and focus on vascular targets or internal organs, the staff is an impact weapon, so your targets need to be susceptible to blunt force trauma.

Basically, a staff strike can be classified as either a distractor or a disabler. Distractors are those attacks that do not themselves debilitate the opponent, such as hand strikes or strikes that target the knees. These strikes create openings and opportunities for you to land a disabling strike to neutralize the opponent. As important as distractors are to your overall strategy, remember that alone they are unlikely to dissuade a determined attacker. Therefore you need to focus on using them to set up and land a solid disabling strike. Disabling strikes, such as a thrust to the face, do more serious damage and prohibit the opponent from continuing the fight.

Strikes can also be classified as either structural attacks or as attacks on the nervous system. Structural attacks aim to break and crush muscles, bones, or joints. Especially susceptible to attack are the knees, hips, shoulders, elbows, and hands. Nerve attacks cause pain, muscle failure, or even unconsciousness. They range from the "dead leg" that results from a strike (or repeated strikes) to the sciatic nerve on the outer edge of the thigh, to knockouts from strikes to the temple or the vulnerable external carotid artery in the pocket of the neck (shoulder to the top of the ear). Some attacks could be classified as both structural and nerve attacks, especially thrusts to the extremely sensitive centerline targets: the eyes, nose, throat, solar plexus, and groin.

Although each strike is generally performed along a prescribed line, your targets will vary and will not always be in the same positions. Therefore we need to understand that each basic strike can also be delivered at slightly different angles. For example, a number-1 strike can target the temple, the pocket of the neck, the point of the shoulder, the elbow, or the hand. A number-2 strike can attack the knee, sciatic nerve, hip, ribs, or elbow. Vertical strikes (numbers 5 and 6, not shown) can attack downward to the crown of the head, the clavicles, the points of the

The unfortunate results of an uncontrolled thrust to the face. Although it temporarily took him out of the fight, Sensei Mike bore it well, as a warrior should.

shoulders, and the hands. Upward vertical strikes (also not shown) can strike the groin, hands, and up under the chin. Horizontal strikes can strike a number of targets stretching from temple to knee and including the elbows and hands. Thrusting strikes (strike 9, represented here by stars) can be used to effectively attack the face, throat, solar plexus, and groin.

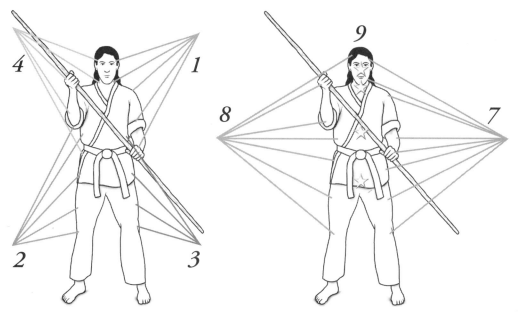

Targets for diagonal strikes.   Targets for horizontal strikes and thrusts.

When attacking, strike the closest available targets. These are usually the hands and the knees. Hand and knee strikes, however, are distractors that may not cause enough structural damage to stop the opponent, so be sure to immediately take advantage of any opening you have created to deliver a decisive disabling blow. Continue attacking available targets from all angles, at all levels, with all the techniques in your arsenal until the opponent has been neutralized. Whenever possible, read the situation and employ restraint, applying the minimum amount of force needed to control the situation. While difficult for the beginner, this becomes more feasible as your ability with the staff increases.

Training Equipment: Target Sticks

Target sticks are important training tools for developing accurate strikes. We use them in much the same way that boxers use focus mitts to develop accurate punches. The difference is that when working with weapons a handheld pad can be too dangerous for the holders due to their close proximity to the weapon. For safety's sake, target sticks extend the holder's reach. While not intended for developing hard strikes, target sticks can provide easily movable targets that will help you develop accurate distancing and precise aim.

To make a target stick, start with a handle (a good use for a broken or beat-up staff). Long sticks are better, at least two feet, as you want to keep your hands well out of range of your partner's strikes, especially early on in his or her training. Wrap the top half of the stick with some sort of padding. An old piece of carpet will work but tends

to be heavy. Foam rubber, especially foam pipe insulation, is light, convenient, and durable. But whatever padding you use, make the end relatively thick so it will not be too hard to hit. Wrap it in several layers of duct or athletic tape for durability, and you are ready to practice.

Try striking the target stick using the basic strikes. Have your partner hold one stick at different levels, and start with simple prearranged patterns (such as low-middle-high or high-high-low-low). Work up to free targeting, with your partner moving two sticks at

random for you to strike. Target holders should retreat, advance, and circle as they slowly change the levels of the target sticks. Concentrate on your form and don't strike too hard. Keep in mind that the purpose of the target sticks is not to develop power but fluid, accurate strikes. Take extra special care not to hit your partner's hands. Just in case, though, your partner should wear some sort of protective hand gear.

You can get creative in your choice of materials for target sticks. I have used all sorts of improvised target sticks with great success. In fact, the black target on the left in the photo of my sticks is just an empty plastic water bottle covered in tape. You are limited only by your imagination and the resources you have at hand.

Combinations

It is rare that a single strike will disable your opponent, so you should attack in well-thought-out combinations. One advantage of a double-ended weapon is the ability to strike to different sides of the body in quick succession, making it difficult for the opponent to block. Initial strikes, however, are often not that hard to see coming. Therefore, a basic strategy should be to strike at one target, drawing a block on that side of the body, and then strike at another target on the opposite side of the body before the opponent can react and redirect the block.

You've been practicing combinations already with the basic strikes. Consecutive strikes with opposite ends of the staff are delivered most efficiently when the staff remains on the same plane. For example, strikes 1 and 2 work well together as a basic combination (see combo 1, below) and can be performed just as effectively when performed in the reverse order as a 2–1 combination. The same can be said for pairing strikes 3 and 4, 5 and 6 (see combo 2), and 7 and 8. Your goal is to be able to put techniques together quickly into effective combinations tailored to meet the specific needs of the situation.

Combo 1: Begin from a middle-grip ready position.

Shuffle forward and deliver strike number 1 to the open pocket of the neck.

If he blocks your first strike, step in with a number-2 strike to the elbow or ribs.

Combo 2: Begin from a middle-grip ready position.

Shuffle forward with strike number 5 to the opponent's exposed head.

If he blocks your first strike, step in with a number-6 strike to the groin.

You are not limited to the combinations of matched pairs as presented in the basic strikes pattern. It can be equally effective to create a combination that attacks both sides of the high line, such as a number-1 strike quickly followed by a number-4 strike (combo 3, below). Similarly, strikes 2 and 3 can be put together to attack both sides of the ribs in quick succession. Each strike should create an opening or otherwise set up your next attack. Don't limit your combinations to only two or three strikes, but keep in mind that shorter combos are easier to remember and implement in combat.

Combo 3: Begin from a middle-grip ready position.

Lunge forward and deliver strike number I to the hand.

Then step in with a number-4 strike downward into the pocket of the neck.

Effective combinations include efficient footwork and target prioritization. Since you begin out of range, you need to slide, shuffle, or step to close the gap and enter striking range. In the example above, combo 3, the opponent's hand is the closest available target. Close the gap with a quick slide forward with the front foot, targeting the hand with a number-1 strike (a distractor) as you close the gap with a full step to attack the right pocket with a number-4 strike (a disabler). Of course, it may take several disabling blows to completely neutralize your attacker and gain full control of the situation.

Combo 4: The opponent's head seems open.

Shuffle forward with a number-1 strike to the pocket of the neck, but it is blocked.

Since the opponent's staff is now vertical, it will be difficult for him to block a vertical strike. Quickly step in with a number-6 strike to the groin.

As a result of the groin strike, the opponent's weapon will be drawn downward. Since you are at close range, retreat a step to reestablish midrange as you deliver a number-5 strike into the pocket of the neck.

Feinting

Smart fighters know the advantages (and disadvantages) of their weapon. They also know techniques that use those advantages to harass and overcome an opponent. As mentioned, one of the advantages of the staff is that it is a double-ended weapon. When it is used properly, your opponent will not know from which side your next strike is coming, which brings us to the topic of feinting.

Feinting is an excellent way to create an opening to score a blow. It begins with what appears to be a fully committed attack; the opponent thinks he sees it coming and reacts. As he does, cut your first technique short in order to launch a second attack from the opposite direction while the opponent is still committed to the defense of the first. Like the basic combinations, basic strikes can be used in matched pairs for feinting. For example, strikes 1 and 2 work well together as a feint/strike combination. They can also be performed in reverse order. The same goes for pairing strikes 3 and 4, 5 and 6, and 7 and 8.

When feinting, stay committed to your initial attack until you see that the opponent is sufficiently committed to his block so that it will be difficult for him to quickly change his plan of action. Then quickly and smoothly change your strike to a second target area. If timed properly, your second strike will come in on the half-beat (as opposed to a full one-two count), giving him no time to react.

If the opponent does not defend against your feint, then it simply becomes a strike.

Feinting: The opponent's head seems open.

Shuffle forward with a number-5 strike, staying committed to the strike only until the opponent is himself committed to blocking it.

Since the opponent's staff is now moving upward to intercept the perceived head strike, it will be difficult for him to stop it and change directions in time to block low. Therefore, discontinue your first strike before completion, quickly stepping in to take advantage of the open lower line with a number-6 strike to the groin.

Strategy and Tactics

In chess, you often hear of masters planning several moves ahead of actual play in order to set an opponent up for a finishing move. This applies to staff fighting as well. But how do you start thinking three or four moves ahead? After all, you can't always predict how your opponent will react. What you need is a strategy that will allow you to predict what your opponent is *likely* to do next and react effectively when he does. A strategy is your overall battle plan. The specific moves you choose to use to implement your plan are called tactics.

While there are an infinite number of strategies to choose from, let's begin with a simple three-step strategy.

1) Attack: Look for an open target on your opponent, and then attack it. If your strike lands, be sure to follow up and quickly finish your opponent (a distractor followed by a disabler). If your opponent blocks, you inadvertently hesitate, or for any other reason do not immediately take advantage of the situation and counterattack, quickly return to your ready, defended position to regroup.

2) Feint/Attack: As soon as possible, attack the same target again. If your strike lands, be sure to follow up and quickly finish your opponent. If you can see that your strike is going to be blocked, turn the initial strike into a feint and attack with the other end of your staff to a vulnerable target on the opposite side of the body. If the opponent successfully blocks both attacks, quickly return to your ready, defended position to regroup.

3) Double Feint / Attack: Should your opponent block both attacks, double up the feint. Feint to your first target, then to second as well, finally committing all of your resources to the third attack.

By developing strategies beforehand, you will be better equipped to deal with an opponent because you have a battle plan, just like the chess master. Your moves are no longer random techniques thrown haphazardly at the opponent, but tactics in a systematic, logical plan to control and overcome the opponent.

At the same time, since all opponents and situations are different, you will need to be flexible and able to adapt your tactics so your strategies will still be effective in any given situation.

Victorious warriors win first and then go to war, while defeated warriors go to war first and then seek to win.
—Sun Tzu, *The Art of War*

Training Equipment: The Pell

A stake was planted in the ground by each recruit in such a manner that it projected six feet in height and could not sway. Against this stake the recruit practiced with his wickerwork shield and wooden stick just as if he were fighting a real enemy. Sometimes he aimed against the head or the face, sometimes he threatened from the flanks, sometimes he endeavored to strike down the knees and the legs. He gave ground, he attacked, he assaulted and he assailed the stake with all the skill and energy required in actual fighting. . . .
—Roman General Flavius Renatus, circa AD 400

In the martial arts, we learn techniques by building "muscle memory" through the long-term repetition of movements. Delivering combinations of cuts and thrusts against empty air is insufficient practice for combat. To develop the strongest and most fluid motions possible, you must train against a striking target.

The pell (from the Latin word *palus,* meaning a pole or stake) is an ancient martial arts training tool that was used throughout the world. Roughly simulating a human body, the pell was traditionally a simple tree trunk or wooden post placed in the ground. The

Japanese pell is called a *makiwara.* Modern variations on the pell include all manner of freestanding and hanging heavy bags, offering a variety of staff training opportunities.

The pell gives the staff fighter the same advantage that a punching bag gives a boxer: it provides a focus target for developing focus, aim, power, and distance. By offering resistance, it enables you to practice your combinations of moves in a more realistic manner not possible when merely striking against the air. Pell training teaches proper striking technique by providing you with immediate feedback on each strike. In order to strike with focused force, your entire body needs to move in concert. You develop this coordination by dodging and traversing with combinations of feints and strikes as you move around the pell.

Although you should eventually focus on power, not striking hard allows you to work on accuracy, proper body mechanics, and footwork. This can lead to faster progress and, ultimately, a deeper understanding of the alignment and structure behind your techniques.

A good yet cheap pell can be made from an eight-foot log or similar long wooden post. Dig a hole about two feet deep, stand the post upright, and secure it in place with quick-drying concrete. Obviously, you cannot bring such a pell inside when it rains, so it will suffer both from the beating you'll give it with your staff and from exposure to the elements. So you can expect it to last only a couple of years.

On the other hand, a freestanding pell, which can be made cheaply using a concrete-filled tire to secure the post, does not require a permanent location, can be moved easily, and therefore may last much longer. To fill the tire, duct tape a plastic bag onto the inside of the bottom to keep the concrete from leaking out when you pour it. The post will stay upright by itself within fifteen minutes of pouring and be hard enough to move after an hour, but try to wait at least five days before hitting it (always the hardest part for me).

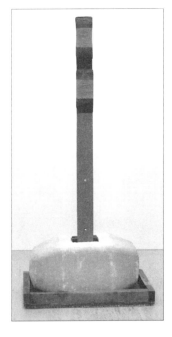

Keep in mind that you may not need to construct anything. Simply look around for a convenient tree, fence post, or telephone pole. You may wish to wrap any living tree in protective padding to prevent injuring it.

Repeatedly hitting any solid wooden post can be hard on both your staff and your body, so consider adding some padding to any pell you use. Not only will your staff last longer, it will also reduce the impact on your joints, and your neighbors won't complain about that loud "Clack! Clack! Clacking!" noise anymore. Old carpeting works well, but you can also use foam rubber or even old towels. Simply strap them on with duct tape and replace as needed. You could also reduce shock and sound by constructing your pell out of soft materials, such as tires or even a length of thick rope.

Although your first reaction to having a target may be to see how hard and fast you can strike, remember that you are training your muscles to naturally execute each technique. Take time to evaluate your structure and alignment. Begin striking the pell slowly with each technique until you know you are doing it correctly. If your strikes feel clumsy or inaccurate, slow down until you can resolve the issue. Vary your attacks, practicing all techniques from all angles and to all levels. Strive to strike deceptively without telegraphing your intent, while concentrating all the energy of the strike into the point of contact. It is very important that you accelerate the staff *through* your target and not just at the target's surface. Just be careful not to break your staff or tear your heavy bag.

A hanging pell has an advantage over a standing pell because it moves dynamically and reacts to your strikes. In fact, probably nothing is better than a common large canvas heavy bag hanging from a long chain or rope.

The bag will "give" more realistically when struck and, unlike a stationary post, can be made to move. To get more swing, hang your bag higher. You can start the bag swinging at first or simply let it swing in reaction to your strikes. The bag will "run away" at times, forcing you to give chase before it reaches the apex of its swing and charges back at you. Having a moving pell is the best way to train for a moving opponent when you have no training partner.

Remember that even if your pell is stationary, you can still improve your footwork and movement by changing your angle of attack, moving in and out of range, and cutting and thrusting from opening to opening (high, low, left, right). In fact, strive to practice every

A small but well-equipped training area.

technique you know on the pell. Practice the accuracy of your thrusts intermingled with your cuts and feints. Develop combinations, building from a simple, direct strike to a logical sequence of techniques. Take the time to properly develop each combination until the techniques become reflexive actions, the result of muscle memory gained through countless repetitions.

Practice regularly and a lot. The pell should be used daily to help improve your physical conditioning and staff technique. Spend time training at the pell wearing all of the possible equipment you might wear while fighting. If you wear a helmet and gloves, spend some time wearing them as you work the pell.

You can also use bungee cords or old karate belts to attach a weapon to your pell. Tying an old staff to a striking post allows you to practice techniques that involve blocking or otherwise manipulating the weapon as you enter. Continually modifying your training and equipment will help avoid the monotony and plateaus that can test the resolve of even the most dedicated athletes.

Defense: The Wall

In level-1 training, diagonal blocks look a lot like diagonal strikes. However, this can leave parts of your body exposed. When blocking, it is important to maximize your available blocking surface by holding your staff perpendicular to the incoming strike, creating a wall between yourself and the opponent's weapon. Block with a forceful counter pulse; don't just sit and wait for the strike to come to you, or it may blow through your block. In fact, purely defensive blocking won't get you far. It may block the current attack, but it does nothing to counter or otherwise stop the next attack. Therefore, offensive blocking, stepping in with the block, allows you to break the attacker's momentum. Blocking perpendicularly to the incoming attack will help keep the opponent's weapon from sliding into your hand.

Perform the blocks stationary at first, then retreating (defensive), advancing (offensive), and finally freestyle (switching the footwork as needed). Advanced students should change the order of the strikes so the blocker learns how to read the setups for each attack. Practice on all sorts of surfaces and in all sorts of environments, in all conditions.

Whenever you learn a particular technique, it is useful to know the counters to it should you ever have to use them or have them used against you. The wall can be defeated by a well-timed feint (as described earlier in "Strategy and Tactics"), drawing the opponent into committing himself to a particular blocking maneuver, only to have you quickly switch the direction of your attack to the unguarded side. You can also defeat the wall with a single-ended technique by cutting around the opponent's weapon. This technique comes from fencing, where you slip tightly around the opponent's weapon in order to slip back in on the other side. Now that you are past the opponent's weapon, nothing lies between you and your target.

Gichin Funakoshi, founder of Shotokan karate, demonstrates blocking with "the wall."

A weakness of the wall is that your hands are exposed on the other side. If your opponent decides to target your exposed hands, or if your hand just happens to get in the way of the strike, your only choice is often to quickly open your hand. Since you need two points of contact to steady the staff, keep the open palm pressed against the weapon to reinforce it. Keeping contact with the staff also reduces the time it takes to re-grab the staff as soon as the danger has passed.

Above are some good examples of the wall block in action. Notice that it is sometimes necessary to open your hand to avoid being hit.

Level-2 Workout

Objectives:

1. To learn proper targeting, distancing, footwork, accuracy, and power to employ the nine basic strikes effectively in combat.

2. To develop precise control in your techniques, allowing you to safely practice them with a partner.

3. To learn the proper use of the wall block (including footwork and timing).

1. Warm-Up: Five to ten minutes of downward figure eights, first slowly then gradually speeding up. Intersperse different strikes into your twirls. Twirl, twirl, STRIKE! Twirl, twirl, STRIKE! Mix in some upward figure eights and basic footwork (forward, backward, side-to-side, circling).

2. Targeting/Control: Perform the nine basic strikes using a partner as your target. Strike close to your partner, but do not make actual contact.

Practice each strike singly at first, then in combinations of two, building up to combinations of three to five techniques.

Primary Targets: Opponent's lead hand and lead ankle.
Secondary Targets: Neck pocket (shoulder to top of ear), elbow, knee.
Thrusting Targets: Face, throat, solar plexus, groin, thigh, foot.

3. Accuracy/Distancing: Perform the basic strikes with a partner to a target stick. First hold the target stick stationary at solar plexus level for all nine strikes. Then hold the target stick at neck level and repeat all nine strikes. Next, hold the target stick at thigh level and repeat all nine strikes. Finally, have the holder vary the level of the target stick on each strike.

4. Power: Practice the nine basic strikes to a pell (heavy bag, post, or tree). Use a sturdy staff and take care not to break it! Perform the strikes singly at first, then in combinations of two, building up to combinations of three to five techniques. Include footwork by starting at a distance, closing the gap, entering with feints and combinations, then exiting on a new angle.

5. Defense: Practice the nine basic strikes and blocks with a partner, now using the wall. Practice stationary, advancing, retreating, and circling.

Continue recording each of your workouts in your training log, including a short synopsis of the material you cover in each session. Set a new goal for yourself, perhaps increasing your minimum number of days or hours each week, or performing the above workout a set number of times (again, I suggest a minimum of ten times). Stay motivated, remain disciplined, be consistent, and work hard. With practice, you will continue to improve your skills and deepen your understanding of staff fighting.

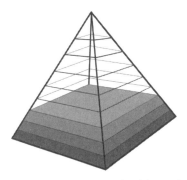

LEVEL 3
Advanced Middle Grip

Level 3 focuses on double striking, hooking disarms, and advanced blocking concepts, such as disarming blocks. It is advisable to wear protective hand gear when practicing disarms, both to protect the hand of the defender and to allow those doing the disarming to use a moderate amount of force in the technique without hurting their partner. Foam-dipped martial arts sparring gear is not recommended because it leaves your thumb exposed (and thumbs get hit a lot in disarming). It is recommended you wear kendo *kote* gloves or similar padded gauntlets like hockey or lacrosse gloves. Other options include heavy welder's gloves or motorcycle gloves with protective plastic plates.

Kendo kote   Gauntlets   Fencing gloves   Lacrosse gloves   Motorcycle gloves

The Double Strike

Double striking allows you to hit the opponent twice with only one swing of your staff. To double strike, you will use a full chambering motion (reminiscent of level 1) to strike with the load-up end of the weapon first, followed by a full strike with the opposite end of the staff. Keep in mind that these are not two separate moves but rather two moves executed as part of a single swing. You can also use a first strike to hook one end of your opponent's weapon, pulling it out of the way to clear a path for the second part of the strike. Don't overly commit to your first attack as it may have a tendency to get snagged or caught up if the target provides strong resistance. You must be ready to switch techniques immediately if your first strike gets stuck, allowing you to flow smoothly into the next best available strike.

Double Strike 1: Start from a standard middle grip.

Shuffle forward, right foot followed closely by the left, as you swing the heel of the staff low across the centerline.

Once across, strike with the heel across the face.

Complete the swing with a number-1 strike to the jaw/neck.

Training Equipment: Target Sticks

As we mentioned, target sticks are training tools for developing accurate strikes. They are also important tools for developing your double-striking skills. How many times can you hit with a single strike? At level 1, the obvious answer is one swing, one hit. At level 2, we learned double striking, bringing the answer up to two hits per swing. However, we can do even better. You are about to learn how to hit four times (or more) to multiple targets in less than one second with just one swing of the staff. Introducing . . . machine gun striking!

Have a partner hold the target sticks at about the distance her hands would be on a staff. Start with the sticks on a vertical line, one above the other. Begin by striking downward, hitting the top target with the heel of your staff. Continue through, striking the bottom target. Continuing your swing, strike the top target with the tip of your staff before following through and hitting the bottom target an instant later. Think "heel, heel, tip, tip."

Your partner holds the target sticks, one above the other, at about the distance her hands would be on a staff.

Strike downward, hitting the top target with the heel of your staff, and continue through, striking the bottom target.

Continuing your swing, strike the top target with the tip of your staff.

Follow through and strike the bottom target.

There is an adage that says, "Know one thing, know a thousand things." Once you know how to strike two targets at once, what could those targets be? Your opponent needs two hands to use his staff, so if he or she were to square up on you, you could immediately target both hands, striking each one twice in less than a second, increasing your odds of landing a solid blow. Or perhaps the targets that present themselves are the head and the lead hand. Or maybe a hand and an overextended lead leg. It is up to you to learn how to recognize the possibilities, first in static, controlled practice with a partner, then incrementally advancing to dynamic freestyle drills using padded staves and proper protective gear.

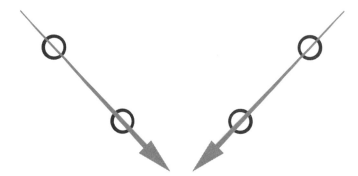

Visualize each strike going through multiple targets.

Once you master machine gun striking, you can use the quick barrage of strikes to quickly overcome an opponent.

Hooking Disarms

Hooking disarms are double strikes that focus on the hands. They consist of hooking one of the opponent's hands with one end of your staff as you follow through and striking the opponent's body with the other end. Because it is not an obvious attack, your opponent often does not perceive the first move as a serious threat until it is too late. When you hook the opponent's hand, it may not be immediately stripped from the weapon. However, if you keep up a steady pressure, potential energy will build in your strike, which can be released into the target when his hand finally slips off. For this reason, be careful when practicing with your partner! Partners should hold firmly but with the knowledge that the harder they hold on, the harder the counterstrike may be. In addition, a full-speed/full-power hooking disarm would likely strike the opponent's hand with a degree of force not safely replicated in controlled practice.

Hooking Disarm 1: Start from a standard middle grip.

Shuffle forward and slip the heel of the staff around the opponent's weapon, hooking inside the lead hand.

Strip the hand and continue through with the motion.

Deliver a number-1 strike to the pocket of the neck.

Hooking Disarm 2: Start from a standard middle grip.

Shuffle forward and drop the tip of your staff, slipping the tip between the opponent's rear hand (the one closest to the heel of the staff) and his weapon.

Strip his hand with a strong, sharp motion.

Follow through with a number-4 strike to the pocket of the neck with the heel of your staff.

This maneuver should be repeated using all of the basic strikes. There are several ways to hook an opponent's hands. You can hook the lead hand or the rear hand, the top of the hand (thumb side) or the bottom, over the top of the staff or under it. Instead of learning every combination as a separate technique, learn the principles of hooking and how to apply them. Perform the hooking disarm drill stationary at first, then advancing, retreating, and finally freestyle.

Although a single successful hook can be all you need to render the opponent's weapon useless (by removing one hand from the weapon), two successive hooks will often result in a complete disarming of the opponent.

The Full Disarm: By combining the previous two hooking disarms into a single series, you can completely disarm an opponent. Start from a standard middle grip.

Shuffle forward to close the gap and slip the heel of your staff around the opponent's weapon, hooking inside the lead hand.

Strip the hand and continue through with the motion.

Deliver a number-1 strike to the pocket of the neck.

Drop the tip of your staff.

Slip the tip of your staff between the opponent's rear hand and his weapon.

Strip his remaining hand with a strong strike.

Follow through with a number-4 strike to the pocket of the neck.

The Push-Pull Energy Drill

This is an exercise for developing strong double strikes and understanding how to effectively apply hooking disarms. Begin by hooking your partner's staff with one end of yours. Press perpendicularly into the center section of your partner's weapon as he provides you with resistance. Keep your elbows down and push and pull hard, but be careful because the potential energy that builds up between your staves can be dangerous to your partner should they slip. Next, slowly make a minor change of angle with your staff, feeling how your staff wants to slide into your partner's hand. Repeat the drill using several different ways of hooking to develop a basic understanding of the technique.

If you feel checked, for example, if your opponent is just too strong to overcome in one direction, then switch and go the other way. Work together to develop the ability to

The Energy Drill: First, lay your staff perpendicularly across your opponent's staff and press straight down. It should be relatively easy for your partner to resist you.

Next, slide your staff to the left until it gently makes contact with your partner's right hand. Pull down and to your left to extend your partner's arm and break his structure.

Do the same thing to his left hand, sliding until you contact the hand, then pulling down and to your right to extend his left arm to unbalance your partner and pull him off his stable base.

smoothly hook the hand and pull your partner off balance in a single, fluid movement. Keep in mind that, when necessary, the hook can be a strike, attacking the hand at the base of the thumb or heel of the hand. This initial strike will add force and momentum to your technique, making your hooking technique far more effective. After practicing this drill, you will know how to disarm quickly and efficiently, and quickly recover should you feel your hook become entangled. Use this drill to fine-tune each of your hooking disarms.

Training Equipment: The Striking Ball

To develop accurate striking techniques, either empty handed or with weapons, a striking ball is a versatile, easy-to-make, and fun piece of training equipment. I started with a single old basketball hung with a piece of rope. For the last decade or so, I have used a pair of striking balls tied to a board hung between two trees to work 360-degree awareness, gain facility at striking moving targets, and simulate fighting multiple opponents.

Sparring sessions with the balls are fast moving and never quite the same, as the balls swing and react differently almost every time they are struck. They have provided me with hours of fun, sweaty, aerobic workouts. Empty handed, I use them to practice punching, kicking, and blocking, moving in and out to develop footwork as well. But I really find them useful in developing good weapons skills, making my strikes fast, accurate, and hard. I have beaten on the striking balls with short sticks, staves, knives, tonfa, nunchaku, bokken, three-sectional staff, and even a spear. In fact, I have worn right through my first striking ball, but I still find it useful, providing a different feel than a new, bouncy striking ball. I strongly recommend that you take this opportunity to spice up your training by adding a striking ball or two to your personal workouts. You won't regret it.

My original striking ball, made in 1990.

The beat-up remains of that same ball over twenty years later, along with its replacement.

To start, you will need to acquire a ball of some sort (I prefer old basketballs for their durability), a length of sturdy rope, and some duct tape. Begin by tying the rope around the middle of the ball, using small pieces of duct tape to hold it in place if needed. Next, wrap a single length of tape around the ball, centered over the rope. Then make two more wraps, one on either side of the rope, overlapping your first length of tape. Finally, place one more layer centered on the rope, just like the first. The result should be a durable, tight wrap that will last a long time.

As a finishing touch, you can secure a spring clip or carabiner to the end of the rope so that you can easily put up and take down your striking ball. Otherwise, you can simply tie your striking ball to a convenient tree limb or other support with sufficient clearance. Now you are ready to rock and roll!

Begin with scissors, duct tape, sturdy rope, a carabiner, and a basketball.

Tie the rope around the middle of the ball, using small pieces of duct tape to hold it in place if needed.

Wrap tape around the ball to secure the rope. Tie the carabiner to the loose end of the rope.

Now you have a striking ball that will last a long time.

Disarming Blocks

It is not enough to merely block an incoming strike. If you do not immediately do something to break the momentum of your opponent's attack, it is likely that he will keep attacking you until he finally succeeds in landing a blow. Therefore, we should strive to take a strategic view of blocking.

The simplest way (and don't be fooled: none of this is easy to pull off in actual combat, at least not at first) is to block the incoming attack by striking the opponent's lead hand as he strikes you (this involves *sen no sen* timing, which will be discussed in more detail in the section "Understanding Timing"). To do this you must be able to see the attack coming and plot the trajectory of the opponent's hand (instantaneously in your head) as you move to intercept it with your staff. These blocks look less like the wall and more like the striking blocks used in level-1 training. Only now, instead of targeting the opponent's weapon, you target the lead hand. Hit with a sharp, hard strike, with the objective of breaking the small bones of the hand and fingers (wear hand protection in practice).

Sometimes, you will only be able to block the weapon. When that happens, you still have options. Immediately after you have succeeded in making the weapon-to-weapon block, slide forcefully along the shaft of the opponent's weapon to strike his hand. This brings us to sliding disarms.

Disarming Blocks: Application to block number 1.

Application to block number 2.

Application to block number 3.

Application to block number 4.

Application to block number 5.

Application to block number 7.

Sliding Disarms

Sliding disarms are executed by sliding sharply down your opponent's staff, striking his hand. Let's say you have just completed a regular block, or you were trying for a disarming block but you missed the hand. This is not uncommon, as the hand is a relatively small target, and your opponent may sense your intention and move his hand at the last second. But this does not mean your attempt was for naught. Maintain contact with the opponent's staff, sliding your staff sharply parallel down the shaft and directly into the opponent's hand, hopefully getting him to release his hold on the weapon. If he does, immediately take advantage of the opportunity by completing the technique and disarming him or attacking other parts of his body.

Parries can also lead into sliding disarms. Once you have attained contact with the opponent's staff, stick to it, sliding your staff along the shaft to impact against the opponent's front hand. A perfect example is the basic block to the number-9 strike that you already know.

Complete the standard vertical parry, but commit only enough motion to your parry to neutralize the opponent's strike.

Quickly switch directions, driving the center of your staff into your opponent's lead hand.

Follow up with a strike to the face.

If you land the hand strike but fail to disarm the opponent, do not fret; you may have done more damage than you think, if only psychological. Try for the same hand again, either with a blocking disarm or with another sliding disarming attack. You may get him to release the hand the second time, but even if for some reason you do not succeed, your efforts will not be wasted, for now you have programmed your opponent to think that you are going to target his hand. On your next attack, feint to the hand. Based on his response to the previous two attacks, strike him instead where you know he will be open. Such application of strategy and tactics separates the novice from the expert in staff fighting.

Sliding Disarm: Your opponent attacks with a number-1 strike, which you block.

Immediately slide down the opponent's staff, striking his lead hand sharply.

Shushi's Wall

The following is a combination I call "Shushi's Wall" (from an Okinawan form called *shushi no kon*). It utilizes the wall block and exemplifies the coordinated use of strategy, footwork, counterattacking, and disarming techniques. On the surface, the basic moves appear pretty simple, but analysis of the potential applications reveals hidden strategies and tactics contained within the combination.

Shushi's Wall: Begin in a ready position.

Drop your lead foot back and lunge away.

Step forward again, blocking from right to left with a wall block.

Counter with a left-to-right horizontal strike to the head.

Follow up with a diagonal strike.

Finish with a forward thrust.

Below are the applications to each move.

Shushi's Wall (applied): You face your opponent in middle grip. A direct attack from the ready position offers little chance of success.

Instead, momentarily drop your lead foot back and leave your left side conspicuously open in an attempt to draw the opponent forward with a right-handed attack.

As soon as you see your opponent move to close the gap you've created between you, step forward again (once the opponent has begun his step, he will be committed to his forward motion until that foot lands), blocking from right to left with a wall block, covering any attack coming from your left.

Immediately counterattack with a left heel strike to the head, parrying his staff in the process.

Follow with a hooking disarm into a double strike.

Finish with a number-1 strike to the pocket of the neck.

Step on the opponent's lead foot, pinning it to the ground, as you thrust forward and down into the pocket of the neck.

Since the front foot is pinned, the opponent is easily taken to the ground.

Level-3 Workout

Objective: To learn proper targeting, distancing, footwork, accuracy, and power to employ double strikes and hooking disarms effectively in combat.

Warm-Up: Five to ten minutes of downward and upward figure eights, first slowly then gradually getting faster, interspersed with different strikes and the wall block. In addition, visualize double striking and performing hooking disarms as you twirl. Incorporate basic footwork: advancing, retreating, and circling.

1. Distancing/Control: Perform the first eight basic strikes, employing the double striking principle and using a partner as your target. Build proper distancing and good control by striking close to your partner but not making contact.

2. Accuracy: Have a partner hold a pair of target sticks about two feet apart. Practice the first eight basic strikes as double strikes, hitting the targets gently at first, concentrating on proper form and accuracy. Gradually build speed, *but never sacrifice accuracy.* Remember that target sticks are for developing accuracy, not power. Wear hand protection.

3. Power: Practice your double strikes to the striking ball(s). You will probably notice that striking or hooking with the heel of the staff can result in a surprisingly powerful blow. You may have to tap rather gently with the heel hook in order to land a double strike on the same ball. Use a sturdy staff, and even then take care not to break it. Fight the striking ball(s), using footwork to maintain distance while evading the balls as they swing. Practice your disarming blocks by visualizing striking an opponent's hands.

4. Hooking Disarm Drill: Execute the first eight strikes as hooking disarms with a partner. Disarm with strike 1, then let your partner re-grab before hooking with a number-2 strike, number-3 strike, and so on, until you have done all eight disarms in quick succession. Partners should not be completely compliant but also should not hold on too tightly. A sharp initial strike will usually loosen the hand but can hurt even through hand gear, so work with your partner to find a safe medium that is as realistic as possible while still preventing injury.

5. Defense: Practice Shushi's Wall, solo and with a partner. First perform the combination solo a minimum of ten times, then repeat with a partner. Start slowly and with good control. Gradually add speed, but take care to not actually strike your partner.

Continue to set short-term goals for yourself.
Work hard, record your workouts, and see results!

Workout

Level-3

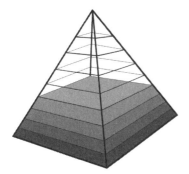

LEVEL 4
Basic Extended Grip

Introduction to Extended Grip

Level 4 introduces extended-grip striking. The advantage of the extended grip is that it allows you to strike your opponent while staying outside his effective striking range, as you can clearly see in the illustration below (and in the circle of death—see the discussion in "Range, Distancing, and the Circle of Death" in level 2).

Despite popular belief, most recorded European staff fighting was done at extended grip, not—as depicted in the Robin Hood films—middle grip. In fact, some theorize that the very name "quarterstaff" comes from

Extended grip versus middle grip; notice the difference in ranges.

the fact that one would grip only *one-quarter* of the staff. (This is not the only explanation. Another is that it was carved from a sturdy length of quartered trunk wood as opposed to a branch.) Staves naturally vary in length, from the short four-foot Japanese *jo* to the ten-foot English lance. While the quarter grip may work well on an eight-foot staff, today's staves are more commonly about six feet long. It is recommended that, with a shorter staff, you adopt a grip on one-third of the weapon, leaving two-thirds extended in front of you to fight with.

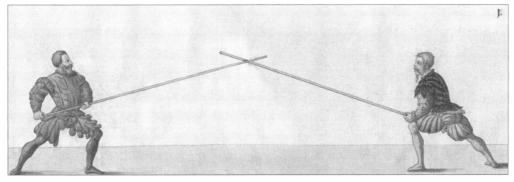

The long staff, from Paulus Hector Mair's *Opus amplissimum de Arte athletica* (The greatest work on the athletic arts), painted by Jörg Breu the Younger, circa 1550.

The low guard was considered the "true guard" for fighting with the staff.

The low guard is the most common fighting stance with extended grip. Your front foot is pointed at your opponent. Sit back onto your rear leg, which is turned out about 90 degrees. Keep both knees bent and your feet about one and a half shoulder widths apart. This provides a solid base while keeping you relatively safe and out of range. Granted, your front leg is open to attack, but since it is not weighted heavily, you should be able to move it quickly. The back stance also chambers your weight for a quick shift into forward stance, an action that closes the gap and gets your body mass moving forward. This is especially useful in combination with a thrusting strike or snap strike (see level 4).

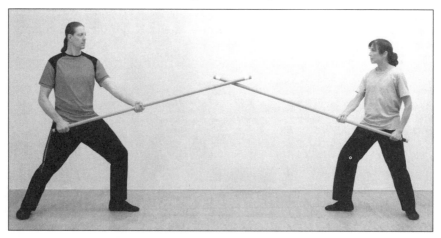

As a general rule, you should hold the centerline by keeping the extended tip aimed at your opponent's face or throat.

As mentioned earlier, since you will frequently be sliding your hands along the staff, you want to be sure to sand off any shiny protective finish your staff may have, as this can greatly hinder switching smoothly from one grip to another. Also, take the time to carefully inspect your staff before each workout by running your hands gently along its length. Feel for splinters that could potentially go into your hand. If you find any, they should be sanded off or taped over.

Using the extended grip with proper distancing allows you to strike your opponent while staying out of range yourself. This is considered long-range fighting. Development of your outside game (so called because you are staying *outside* of your opponent's effective range) is crucial to smart fighting and the proper implementation of the Grand Overall Strategy presented later in level 6.

To that end, you should always remember to look for the chance to strike the front leg because most people leave it too far out and therefore exposed. Use extended strikes to your opponent's unguarded weak points to develop your attack assessment (i.e., how you can best proceed). You have a higher likelihood of seeing and striking an undefended target, resulting in a higher likelihood of getting that psychologically important first hit.

Slip in the knee shot before the opponent can react to your sudden switch to extended grip.

Extended-Grip Basic Strikes

While the strength of the extended grip is in its superior reach, its weakness lies in the tendency to focus on using only one end of the weapon. If you do that, you have traded the advantage of having a double-ended weapon for one with greater range. But why not have *both*? You can. Drilling the nine basic strikes while alternating the striking end of your weapon on each strike will teach you how to flow smoothly along the staff, allowing you to continue striking with both ends of the weapon even at maximum range. The series below includes chamber positions.

Extended-Grip Figure Eights

Figure eights are a great way to practice repeated diagonal strikes in extended grip as well as middle grip. Practice upward figure eights as well. Extended-grip figure eights can be a great exercise for building the muscles in your wrists, forearms, upper arms, shoulders, and back.

For a practical application for the extended-grip figure eight, look no further than the fierce Donga fighters of the Surma tribe in Ethiopia. Donga is a form of full-contact staff fighting: part martial art, part ritual, part spectator sport. Fights are used to settle vendettas, solve disputes, and earn wives, so it should be no surprise that fighters are very competitive and risk serious injury and occasionally even death. Matches are fought nude (or nearly so) with minimal armor. Fighters occasionally wear headgear, forearm protectors, shin guards, and very small bucklers to protect the hands, all made from cloth or wicker.

Donga fighters hold their staves in extended grip, and often use a circular technique that is closely related to the extended-grip figure eight. The staff first parries the opponent's attack with a technique known in different systems as a hanging block, wing block, or roof block, followed by a speedy downward strike. The downward swing could also be used to beat the opponent's weapon down, followed by another speedy downward strike. Variations include horizontal strikes and a version using upward figure eights as well. These techniques are combat proven and therefore well worth studying. The drill below was inspired by Donga fighting.

The Donga Drill: Your partner begins with a vertical downward extended strike aimed at your head.

Step offline slightly as you block overhead with a hanging block.

Deflect your partner's staff downward.

Raise the staff over your head and begin your own downward strike.

Your partner then steps slightly offline and blocks overhead with a hanging block.

As the opponent strikes again, repeat the drill. Keep in mind that you should not continually block on the same side. You can block to either side, stepping offline to the left or right, depending on which block you use.

Extended-Grip Thrusting

When you are in the basic ready position using the extended-grip guard (low guard), it is important to keep your weapon on your centerline to protect from incoming attacks. From this position you can take full advantage of your control of the centerline as well as the length of your staff by thrusting straight forward into the opponent. These attacks are faster than arcing swings because they are linear, making them shorter and more difficult to block than full swings. However, since their path is short, it is harder to build up speed, so thrusts depend on a body shift for power.

There are basically two ways to thrust: a fixed-hand thrust jabbing with both hands held stationary on the staff, or by sliding the staff through your front hand and driving it with the rear hand only, which is called a slip thrust or a "pool cue" strike. In either case, you will need to get momentum behind the strike. Start in a back stance and shift your weight forward as you strike, lending power to the thrust with the movement of your body mass. To maximize speed and power, add in a rotational force, snapping your rear hip forward sharply into the strike. Transfer the energy around your torso and diagonally across your back, driving the rear shoulder forward. This will power the driving hand and ultimately the staff itself.

With proper distancing, the back stance can keep you just out of your opponent's range but at the edge of your own thrusting range when you shift into the forward stance. The slip thrust is quicker and has a greater range, but it tends to lack the power of the fixed-hand thrust. Therefore, slip thrusts are useful for attacking vulnerable areas such as the face or throat but usually won't cause serious damage to other, more durable target areas.

Practice striking low, targeting the top of the thigh; middle, to the solar plexus; and high, to the throat and face. You can also thrust with the heel as well as the tip of your staff.

Training Equipment: The Target Ball

To develop precise striking and thrusting, practice against a target ball. It is made from a ball attached to a string, and you simply hang it up and get poking!

You have many options when making a target ball. To string a tennis ball, make two one-inch slits on opposite sides of the ball with a sharp utility knife. Tie a knot in the end of your rope (clothesline is ideal) large enough that it will not slip through the closed slit. Squeeze the ball to open the slits enough to thread the rope through. Pull until the knot is on the bottom of or even inside the ball. The ball I am using in the picture below is made of foam, so I stuck a piece of thick wire through the ball with a hook on the bottom to keep it from coming off. Then I simply bent the top into an eye using a pair of needle-nosed pliers and tied the string to that. The other ball in the photo is just a big knot in the end of the rope and covered in red duct tape. In fact, almost any type of small, durable, mobile target would do as a striking ball.

Start by thrusting at a stationary target, then practice hitting the ball as it gently swings from side to side. Work your way up to the point where you can consistently hit the ball with a thrust regardless of its motion. Do not just limit yourself to thrusting attacks, as the target ball can be used to practice your other strikes as well. Hang several balls to develop your multi-targeting skills. Remember that the objective with the target ball is not to deliver a forceful strike. That type of training is better left to pell work. Rather, use the target ball to refine your technique, honing the accuracy of your thrusts and strikes.

Training Equipment: The Thrust Board

The target ball will develop accuracy in your thrusts, but to develop power you will need a more resistant target. The thrusting board is a simple pell made from a piece of wood positioned to mimic the angle of an opponent's front leg and body. A five-foot section of $2'' \times 6''$ treated pine works very well. Drawing or painting small circles on the board will give you targets for honing the accuracy of your thrusts.

As with extended-grip thrusting, practice striking low, targeting the top of the thigh; middle, to the solar plexus; and high, to the throat and face. You will find that slip thrusts are quicker and have better range, but have little force behind them when compared with the fixed, two-handed thrust. Therefore, they are useful for attacking vulnerable areas such as the face or throat but usually won't cause serious damage to other, more durable target areas.

As we mentioned, practice delivering thrusting strikes from middle grip as well. Of course, the range is much less, so you will have to get closer to the target, but then you gain the option of delivering thrusting

strikes with the heel of the staff as well. Like tip thrusts, heel thrusts can be delivered with two hands fixed on the staff or as slip thrusts. Either way, strike fast, like a cobra or rattlesnake, returning quickly to a guarded position, immediately ready to follow up or attack again.

Working the thrust board can get tedious, but you can relieve some of the monotony by setting goals like striking one hundred times, or by playing music and striking in rhythm to a song, or by making a game of it. Simply paint several different colored targets on your thrust board, then have a partner say a color at random and you hit the corresponding target. The targets could also be numbered. Use your imagination to keep your training fun and enjoyable!

A low thrust intended to land just above the knee.

Snap Strikes

Snap strikes are short, sharp blows delivered without the aid of a load-up or chamber position. Since they lack the momentum of a full strike, they must rely on speed and proper leverage for power. Hip rotation and torqueing or wringing the hands is essential to adding sharp focus to a strike. Combine this with a forward shift, and the result looks like a thrust with a sharp snap at the end. With practice you can deliver a snap strike on any angle. Since there is very little telegraphing involved, snap strikes are an excellent way to attack the opponent's hands, leaving him little time to react before he is struck.

Downward Snap Strike: In a single coordinated movement, push with your left hand and pull with your right, wringing the hands down and in as you shift your weight to your lead foot. Notice the increase in reach without moving your feet.

Upward Snap Strike: Push down with your right hand and pull up with your left, wringing your hands as you shift your weight to your lead foot. Again, notice the extended range on the strike.

Training Equipment: The Horizontal Makiwara

When practicing vertical snap strikes, it is especially helpful to have a horizontal target that offers you a good angle to develop snap and power. While a makiwara or pell of this sort can be made from a thick branch or a thin log, I chose to use bamboo from my backyard.

First, I laid the stalks of bamboo across two chairs.

Then I bound the bundle together with duct tape and trimmed the ends to the same length using a circular saw. Wear eye protection and always be careful using power equipment.

In order to keep the bundle tightly wrapped and to give my bamboo makiwara a finished look, I wrapped it in the middle and at each end with some old karate belts and thin clothesline-style rope.

Finally, I hung my new training tool between two trees and got busy snap striking (below). I also use it to practice thrusts and other techniques, too.

Be creative; you are limited only by your imagination!

A horizontal striking surface is perfect for honing your snap strikes.

Extended-Grip Blocking Disarms

Extended-grip blocking should target the opponent's front hand whenever possible. Since the block lacks real strength at this distance, you are essentially striking the opponent utilizing the force of his own strike against him. Therefore, accuracy and good timing are of prime importance. Break an opponent's fingers, and he will have a difficult time holding on to, let alone fighting with, the staff.

If you find you are not close enough to hit an opponent's hands, the opponent probably can't hit yours, either. In that case the opponent may attack your weapon, either out

An example of a well-placed and well-controlled
extended-grip block.

of inexperience or in an attempt to create an opening; if so, exploit this error. Rather than trying to block and stop the force of the attack midstrike, use the end of your extended staff to parry the strike, keeping the momentum of the technique. This, combined with subtle offline movements, allows you to momentarily take control of the opponent's weapon and redirect it where *you* want it to go. If you can direct the strike downward, it is possible to briefly pin your opponent's weapon to the ground, clearing a line along which you can launch an effective counterattack. Quickly take advantage of such an opening with a sharp strike to the opponent's lead hand or body!

Level-4 Workout

Objective: To learn proper targeting, distancing, footwork, accuracy, and power to employ extended-grip striking and blocking effectively in combat.

1. Warm-Up: Five to ten minutes of middle- and extended-grip figure eights, first slowly and gradually getting faster, interspersed with different strikes. Practice smoothly switching from extended grip to middle grip and back again. Incorporate basic footwork: advancing, retreating, and circling. Visualize doing the Donga drill, blocking as you sidestep, then countering with a powerful downward strike.

2. Distancing/Control: Perform the nine basic strikes in extended grip using a partner as your target. Start slowly, developing proper distancing and good control by striking close to your partner but not making contact.

3. Striking Accuracy: Have a partner hold a pair of target sticks. Practice the nine basic strikes in extended grip, hitting the targets gently at first and concentrating on proper form and accuracy. Gradually build speed but never at the expense of accuracy. Remember that target sticks are for developing accuracy, not power. Your partner should wear hand protection.

1. First hold the target stationary at solar plexus level for all nine strikes.

2. Then hold the target at neck level and repeat all nine strikes.

3. Next, hold the target at thigh level and repeat all nine strikes.

4. Finally, have the holder switch the target level on each strike.

4. Thrusting Accuracy: Practice thrusting to a target ball. Start with the ball stationary at first, then practice hitting the ball as it gently swings from side to side. Work your way up to the point where you can consistently hit the ball with a thrust regardless of its motion. Practice thrusting from both middle and extended grips, and with the heel as well as the tip of the staff.

5. Power: Practice your extended strikes to a pell (heavy bag, striking post, or tree), striking balls, target balls, or thrusting board. Use a sturdy staff, and even then take care not to break it! Fight the equipment, using footwork to close, evade, and step offline as you strike. Practice your disarming blocks by visualizing striking an opponent's hands. Learn to become absorbed in your training, like a moving meditation. Start with five- to ten-minute sessions, working up to twenty to thirty minutes, or even longer.

6. Donga Drill: Practice the Donga drill with a partner. Start slowly and with good control. Gradually add speed, but take care to not actually strike your partner. Incorporate basic footwork: advancing, retreating, and circling. You may wish to wear hand protection for this exercise.

Stay motivated. Continue setting goals and recording your workouts!

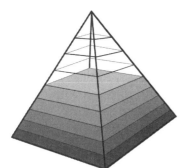

Advanced Extended Grip

Fencing with the Staff

There is much knowledge that we can adapt from fencing for use in extended-grip staff fighting. When you sit back into a back stance and hold the staff in extended grip, your position becomes similar to that of a fencer in a classic on-guard position, albeit with an unusually long sword. The tip of your staff mirrors the tip of a fencer's foil.

In the fencer's stance the knees are bent, feet about one and a half shoulder widths apart, with the front toes pointing at the opponent. In karate, it is commonly known as a back stance. From the back stance, you can maneuver until you see an opportunity to attack, then shift into a forward stance to close the gap and land a strike.

The first rule of fencing is to maintain proper distancing. This means staying just outside the opponent's range until the right moment, then entering to quickly land a strike without being struck yourself. This is just as important when fighting with the staff.

Another important aspect of fencing is covering your centerline. As with a fencer's sword, keep your staff aimed at your opponent's throat to prevent him from entering striking range

without having to first either move or get around your weapon. If he attempts to give up the center to deliver an arcing strike, thrust forward quickly and your straight-line technique should land first. In fencing, this is called the straight thrust and is usually accompanied by a deep forward lunge with the front foot; however, the staff requires two hands to wield, so your lunge forward will probably not be as long.

Other techniques from fencing, such as the disengage, cutover, and beat, are used to help you open up clear lines of attack.

A comparison between a fencing stance and the standard low guard.

The Change of Engagement

The change of engagement is another basic concept from classical Western fencing that entails separating ever so slightly from, and circling around, your opponent's weapon in order to create an open line of attack. It is used when your staff makes contact with your opponent's weapon and he pushes against your staff in an effort to control it.

To perform a change of engagement, you must be sensitive to changes in pressure on your staff. As soon as you feel your opponent's staff pressing on yours, relax and make a tight circular motion with the tip of your staff around his weapon to take the centerline. Keep your lead hand still, using it as a fulcrum, as your rear hand makes a circle to slip the tip of your staff under your opponent's weapon and pop it up on the other side. There is no time or space to chamber for a full strike, so you must execute a snap strike or thrust immediately after circling and before your opponent reacts with a block or attempts to reclaim the center.

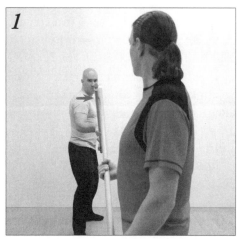

The Change of Engagement: Your opponent is putting pressure on your staff.

Relax, letting the tip of your staff slip under the opponent's weapon.

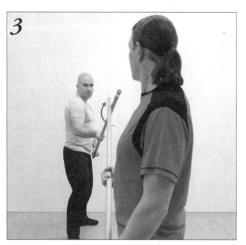

Complete a tight circle, coming up on the freshly exposed line.

Deliver a sharp snap strike to the hand or thrust to the face.

The Double Change

Hockey great Wayne Gretzky once said, *"I skate to where the puck is going to be, not where it has been."* Whether you fight with the staff or do any other competitive activity, you need to be smarter than your opponent, anticipating what your opponent will do ahead of time and acting accordingly.

The double change consists of a combination of two changes of engagement performed in quick succession. Your first disengage is actually a feint. It causes the opponent to over-block

The Double Change: Your opponent is putting pressure on your staff.

Relax, letting the tip of your staff slip under the opponent's weapon.

Complete a tight circle, coming up on the freshly exposed line.

As the opponent cuts back to cover the threatened line, smoothly cut under his staff again. When done correctly and with good timing, the opponent will not even touch your staff.

Finish with a sharp snap strike to the hand

or thrust to the face.

in an attempt to protect his threatened line. When he does, you perform a second disengage, returning to your original line of attack. Don't worry about touching the opponent's staff. If you counter quickly with a thrust or snap strike, your opponent will have trouble blocking or reclaiming the center.

The Cutover

The cutover is similar to the disengage except that, instead of passing the tip of your staff under the opponent's weapon, you go over the tip of his staff to take the inside line. You must move quickly, rising up only enough to clear his tip, delivering a snap strike or thrusting attack along the open line before your opponent can parry your attack.

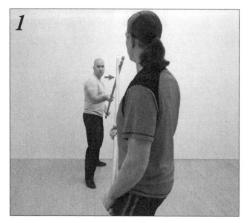

The Cutover: Your opponent is covering his centerline. Press slightly to get him to reply with sideways pressure against your staff.

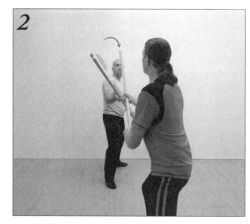

Suddenly relax and make an inverted U-shaped hook, slipping your staff just over the tip of the opponent's weapon.

Attack with a snap strike along the exposed line, hitting the closest exposed target, the lead hand.

The Beat

Beating entails striking the opponent's weapon in order to disrupt his defenses and open up a viable line of attack. To beat the opponent's staff, hit it with a quick, sharp snapping strike. For maximum effect, strike to the weakest part of the opponent's staff, hitting as close to the end of the staff as possible. Hitting near the hands doesn't work as well for two reasons: the staff is stronger structurally there, and the strike results in less movement of the opponent's staff. Don't overcommit when executing a beat, since you will have but an instant to take advantage of the opening you create.

The Beat: Your opponent is covering his centerline.

Strike the opponent's staff suddenly and sharply, knocking it off the centerline.

Immediately switch directions.

Attack with a snap strike along the freshly exposed line of attack, hitting the closest exposed target, the lead hand.

Extended-Grip Hooking Disarms

Extended-grip hooking disarms differ from the middle-grip hooking disarms because they do not rely on strength. Extended-grip hooking disarms lack power, so they rely on finesse to lever the staff smoothly out of the opponent's hands. The extended hook comes in two forms: the hook over and the hook under.

To execute a hook over, you slip your staff over your opponent's staff, slipping the tip under their wrist. Extend the opponent's arm as you make a tight circle, levering against the wrist and stripping his hand from the weapon. It is important that this maneuver be performed in one firm, fluid movement. When you hook over, use a clockwise turn against the right hand and a counterclockwise turn if you hook the left.

If the tip of the opponent's staff is pointed up, it may be easier to hook under the staff and on top of the wrists before making your disarming circle. When attacking the right hand with an under hook, use a counterclockwise circle, and when attacking the left hand, use a clockwise circle.

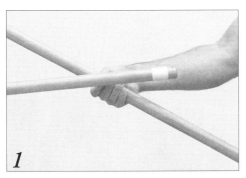

Hook Over Lead Hand: Strike the opponent's hand with an extended strike.

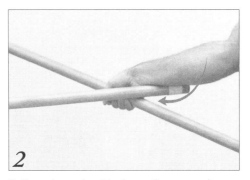

Follow through with the strike, extending his front arm and hooking inside the wrist.

Continue the motion as you pull and lift the hand.

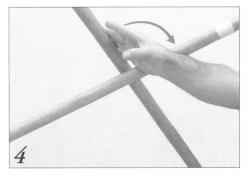

Complete a clockwise circle with the tip of your staff to pry the opponent's fingers from his staff, completing the technique.

Hook Over Rear Hand: Face your opponent in middle-guard extended grip.

Beat the opponent's staff down and to the side with a short, sharp snapping strike.

Use the rebound from the strike to redirect the motion of your staff, smoothly slipping the tip under your opponent's newly exposed rear hand.

Continue in a counterclockwise circle, hooking inside his wrist and extending the rear arm.

Flow with the clockwise circle until your opponent's rear hand slips from the staff.

To complete the technique, quickly switch the direction of your movement, striking the opponent's staff and knocking it to the ground.

Hook Under Lead Hand: Face your opponent in an extended grip. Lower your guard and slip your tip under his staff smoothly. This is best done with a slight offline movement.

Lift the opponent's staff by hooking up under his wrist and extending his arm forward and up on a 45-degree angle.

Flow in a counterclockwise motion until the opponent's staff is driven into the ground.

Continue the motion to completely strip the weapon out of the opponent's hand.

Continue your counterclockwise circle.

Strike the opponent across the head.

The Disarm Drill

The disarm drill is an extension of the push-pull drill you learned at level 3. Martial artists and fighters rely on muscle memory gained through countless repetitions of techniques. But sometimes practicing an entire series of movements is unnecessary and time consuming. Instead, you can focus on specific areas of need, practicing parts of a longer combination of moves in isolation. This allows you to concentrate on the parts you really need to work on. Because it bypasses the opening phase of entering, as well as the final phase of countering, the disarm drill allows you to get in many repetitions of the hooking disarm in a relatively short period of time, building natural, fluid movement through muscle memory.

The Disarm Drill: Start by facing your partner in middle grip.

Slip the tip of your staff over your partner's staff and under his left wrist.

Continue in a counterclockwise circle, pulling to extend his arm.

Complete the disarm.

As your partner re-grabs his staff, drop the tip of your staff smoothly inside his right wrist.

Continue in a clockwise circle.

Complete the disarm.

Begin the sequence again, slipping the tip of your staff inside your partner's left hand. The final motion looks like a mini figure eight. Repeat the drill over and over again, gradually working your way down the staff, until you are performing the hooking disarms smoothly in full extended grip.

When you feel you have adequately mastered the drill above, investigate the many other variations of hooking disarms available against that same guard. Then have your partner switch guards and see what hooking disarms you can find. You can even try executing hooking disarms with the *heel* of your staff. In the end, you should be able to perform a hooking disarm against either hand, from nearly any position, and with either end of your staff.

Training Equipment: Spinners

A spinner is a pinwheel-like training tool mounted to a wall, post, or tree. By turning the spinner repeatedly, you will develop the fine motor control necessary to make tight, controlled circles with the end of your staff. My first spinner was made from a round plastic lid with two paint stirrers attached, but nowadays I cut them out of thin plywood. Use a large nail or screw with a spacer on the back to allow for free movement of the wheel; a short piece of plastic pipe or rubber tubing works well.

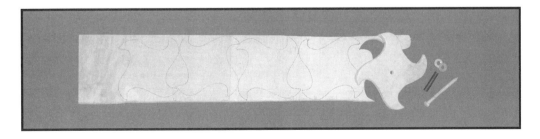

At first, make circles by moving your front hand, then by moving only your rear hand. The stationary front hand helps to disguise the fact that you are initiating a move, whether it be a cut under to take the line or a setup for an extended disarm.

A set of four eight-inch wooden spinners screwed to a post.

You can also use a small hoop to practice your small circles. Spin it on the end of your staff. You could make a hoop out of a variety of materials, including a piece of old hose. Glow necklaces work well and are especially fun to spin in the dark.

Parrying

Blocking is a defensive maneuver that momentarily stops the action by blocking the forward momentum of your opponent's weapon. Parrying is the action of smoothly redirecting the momentum of the opponent's weapon in order to defend or open a line of attack.

The hanging block used in the Donga drill (level 4) is actually somewhere between a block and a parry. Sometimes the opponent's weapon hits nearly perpendicular to your staff. In such a case, the incoming force is brought almost to a complete stop. If the opponent's staff impacts your staff on a greater angle, it tends to glance off and be safely redirected to the side. Because the opponent's weapon keeps moving, the technique is a parry, not a block.

Parry by intercepting the opponent's staff, then redirecting it—up, down, or to either side—off its intended line of attack. Parrying upward is dangerous, however. Whenever you hold the tip of your staff low, you expose your high line and are forced to parry upward from below. This can result in the unfortunate possibility of parrying a thrust to your midsection up and into your own face. It is much safer to parry to the sides, which allows you to redirect the strike clear of your body with the smallest motion, since your body is thinner than it is tall. Of the sides, it is safer to parry to the your right (from a left-leading guard), thereby keeping your staff between you and the opponent's weapon, as opposed to parrying to your left, where an incomplete parry could lead the strike directly into the left side of your body.

Sideways Parry: Keep the tip of your staff pointed at the opponent's throat or face. This effectively closes your high line to attack while keeping the opponent's staff to the right side of your staff, protecting your otherwise exposed left flank.

When the opponent thrusts, parry his weapon sideways just enough that he no longer has an open line of attack.

Parrying downward has the advantage of clearing your opponent's target-rich upper line for attack. You also have the benefit of being able to use the ground to momentarily pin or at least control and restrict your opponent's weapon.

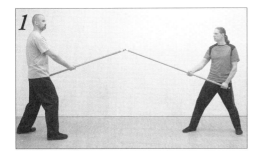

Downward Parry: Keep the tip of your staff pointed at the opponent's throat or face. This effectively closes the high line to attack. The only path available to your opponent is your slightly open lower line.

When the opponent thrusts, parry his attack.

Swat his weapon downward.

While his staff is still moving downward, disengage and counter with a thrust to the face along the open line.

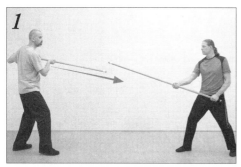

Oar Block: Although this technique is commonly referred to as a block, in this application it is a parry as it does not stop the momentum of the opponent's staff. Start from a standard extended guard.

As the opponent thrusts at you, drop the tip of your staff.

Parry the opponent's weapon with the center section.

As the opponent's staff is redirected safely past you, step forward, continuing the circular motion, striking the opponent with the tip of your staff. Notice how the circular motion is centered on your front hand, which is acting as the fulcrum for the technique.

Part the Grass to Find the Snake

While most extended-grip techniques are best performed with small circles, part the grass to find the snake is a Chinese technique performed with a large circular motion.

Part the Grass to Find the Snake: Begin squared off in extended grip.

Start by angling subtly off the opponent's line of attack, gently intercepting his staff, establishing contact, then parrying it downward and to the outside with a smooth circular motion.

Continue moving your staff in a counter-clockwise circle.

Bring the opponent's staff back to the inner line as you spiral it directly into his face. Your lead hand acts as the fulcrum, making your staff a class-1 lever (see appendix I: "Fighting Physics: The Mechanics of the Staff").

When done correctly, there is a good chance that you can trap the opponent's weapon against his body. Even if you miss the trap, you should still be able to land a solid strike.

Coupled with solid footwork, you can use this technique to take your opponent to the ground. Put your rear hand on your hip, using it as the new fulcrum, creating a class-2 lever with your staff (again, see appendix I). Press downward with your lead hand, wringing your hands as you press your staff down and across your opponent's chest, driving him slightly backward. This will lock up your opponent's spine and prevent him from stepping backward and regaining his base. This compromises his overall structure and allows you to drive him backward and to the ground with relatively little energy.

Level-5 Workout

Objective: To acquire and apply basic fencing skills with the staff in extended grip.

1. Warm-Up: Five to ten minutes. Practice making small circles with the tip of the staff. Do mini figure eights with the tip, first slowly, then gradually getting faster. Intersperse little snap strikes into your twirls. Twirl, twirl, STRIKE! Twirl, twirl, STRIKE! Try upward figure eights and add basic footwork. You can also use spinners or hoops if available.

2. Distancing/Control: Perform the nine basic strikes as short snap strikes to the air. Then perform the nine basic snap strikes using a partner as your target. Strike close to your partner, but do not make actual contact. Primary targets: opponent's lead hand and lead ankle. Secondary targets: neck pocket (shoulder to top of ear), elbows, knees. Thrusting targets: face, throat, solar plexus, groin, thigh, foot.

3. Accuracy/Timing: Alternate doing the following combinations with a partner: (1) disengage; (2) double disengage; (3) cutover; (4) beat and straight thrust; (5) beat, feint straight thrust, disengage, straight thrust; and, finally, (6) create your own combinations.

4. Power: Perform the nine basic snap strikes to a pell (heavy bag, post, or tree). Develop short, sharp power without telegraphing by chambering. Because it is extremely durable and provides the perfect target for both upward and downward snap strikes to the hand, the hanging horizontal bamboo *makiwara* (see "Training Equipment: The Horizontal Makiwara" in level 4) is especially suited for this training. Once you have developed power, begin striking to the inside of a tire. Hung vertically, the tire will restrict your pull-back motion, helping you develop very short, powerful strikes.

5. Disarm Drill: Execute the first eight strikes as hooking disarms with a partner. Disarm with strike 1, then let your partner re-grab before hooking with a number-2 strike, number-3 strike, and so on, until you have done all eight disarms in quick succession. Partners should not be completely compliant, but should not hold on too tightly, either. A sharp initial strike will usually loosen the hand but can hurt even through hand gear. So work with your partner to find a safe medium that is as realistic yet as safe as possible. Repeat the drill, gradually working your way down the staff until you are performing the hooking disarms smoothly in full extended grip.

6. Part the Grass: Practice the combination *part the grass to find the snake* with a partner a minimum of ten times each. No partner? No problem! Try fastening a long staff to your pell with some bungee cords. Even with the tip hanging to the ground, you will still get a feel for manipulating your opponent's staff.

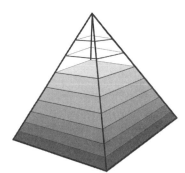

LEVEL 6
Combat with the Staff

The Moment of Truth

If you've trained hard and learned the lessons from levels 1–5, then it is time to see how well it works against an actual opponent. Level 6 focuses on putting together everything you've learned into effective fighting combinations, then repetitively practicing those combinations until they are ingrained and can be performed automatically as the situation warrants. This is the level at which a student begins to develop his or her own personal fighting method with the staff.

It is not unusual for sparring with the staff to feel awkward at first. There is a big difference between doing drills with a partner and the chaos of combat against a noncompliant opponent who is trying his best to hit you. Stick with it. Your techniques may not work well at first. You *will* get hit. Often. Sometimes it will hurt. Deal with it. Open yourself to the thrill that comes with training in combat sports, the satisfaction of overcoming hardships, and the confidence that comes with knowing that your techniques will actually work for you should you need them.

En garde!

Full-Contact Fighting

There are several different methods for safely honing your weapons skills against actual opponents in mock combat without holding back very much, if at all. The secret lies in the proper combination of two key components: good protective gear and properly padded weapons. Over the past decade, I have created many prototypes of padded weapons and experimented with many types of armor, testing them all in hours of brutal full-contact combat. Here is what I have learned: padded weapons, especially staves, are best made at home from easily acquired materials, while the best armor is usually hockey, lacrosse, or eskrima gear. I will go over padded weapons construction first, since it is safest and requires a minimal amount of equipment. Then we will take a look at the best available armor, so you can eventually work up to full-contact sparring with unpadded rattan staves.

My first pugil sticks had a sturdy wooden staff as a core. They were padded on each end with open-cell foam rubber covered with duct tape. The wooden core proved too heavy, the open-cell foam did a lousy job of cushioning the blow, and the unpadded center section wasn't much fun in close-quarters combat. Long story short, my latest designs feature a PVC core covered completely with closed-cell pipe insulation, with thick foam striking caps on each end. These endcaps are a key safety feature that I came to understand the importance of only after one of my students received three stitches across the bridge of his nose from a thrust to the face (see the photo in "Targeting" in level 2).

At first I wore no protective gear at all (ugh . . . caveman no need armor!), but you don't need to get smacked in the groin too many times with a padded staff before you learn the value of wearing a cup. I gradually added padding to my elbows, knees, hands, and head (not necessarily in that order). One of the advantages of wearing a lot of armor or protective sports gear is that you can start to fight with non-padded rattan staves.

With well-padded sticks you can spar wearing only a fencing or eskrima mask, a cup, and a pair of padded gloves. Foam hand gear used in karate was not designed for holding a weapon, so it leaves your thumb exposed and vulnerable to injury. If the staves are sufficiently padded, welder's gloves may be enough to ward off the sting of most blows. Lacrosse and hockey gloves offer excellent hand protection, but even these can sometimes leave your fingers open to hard strikes. Goalie gloves are specially designed with more padding, especially on the vulnerable thumb.

An example of the armor required for full-contact fighting with unpadded staves.

Open-faced foam karate sparring headgear is useless against any blows to the face. Fencing headgear protects the vulnerable face area and is easy to breathe through (very important when you're huffing and puffing in the middle of a fight), but most provides little protection against strikes to the sides and top of your head. Eskrima headgear, on the other hand, is padded all the way around, and provides more protection than a typical fencing helmet.

In the end it is important that you experiment with different types of protective gear, pads, and armor (forearms, elbows, knees, and body) until *you* feel adequately safe and protected.

Which brings us to the fight. Remember, this is just *mock* combat, and no amount of padding or protective gear can make up for a good temperament, good technique, and good control. The fact is that injuries can occur in any activity that involves physical contact, and even more so when fighting with weapons. Remember always that you are not out to actually hurt your partner (at least I should hope you are not!), so don't. Discuss how hard a hit you are each comfortable with, as well as other rules, such as *no punching or kicking, stop if the fight ties up or goes to the ground, or only controlled takedowns.*

Start out fighting slowly and with little power. Such fighting is good as both a mental and physical warm-up, and it gives you an opportunity to feel out your opponent. After a few moments, you can gradually step it up a little until you are fighting at an intensity level agreeable to both combatants. Always keep your head and never lose your cool, even when things get hectic. Take your weapons and the fight seriously, always keeping in your mind that, if these were real weapons, even a single blow, especially a shot to the hand, could decide everything. Training with such a mindset will improve your weapons skills much more quickly than a "hit them more than they hit me" attitude. Remember that good defense is essential. Try to anticipate where your opponent will strike you and then block or move out of range, but keep in mind that defense alone will not win a fight. As for specific fighting tactics, stay flexible and continually adapt to the ever-changing circumstances of the fight.

Breaking a staff during sparring while training
for the 2014 World Championships in Hungary.

Training Equipment: The Padded Staff

Start with a six-foot length of three-quarter-inch PVC pipe. Tape or glue a light duty
rubber cap to each end (step 1). Heavy endcaps like those used for a cane or a walking
stick hurt more, so don't use them. Next, carefully cover the entire length of the staff
with closed-cell pipe insulation (step 2).

Cut this layer even with the ends of the weapon, and then cut several foam disks the
same diameter as the end of the padded weapon (step 3). Affix at least three of these disks
on each end with strips of duct tape to create a padded thrusting tip that does not allow
the rubber stopper on the end of the PVC to make contact with a target (step 4).

Next, wrap an additional layer of larger-diameter closed-cell pipe insulation or other
foam around the top and bottom third of the weapon, leaving the middle third with only
a single layer of foam to make for an easier grip (step 5).

Carefully wrap the entire length with duct tape, making sure not to compress the
foam more than necessary. A tightly wrapped stick does not allow the foam to absorb the
impact of a strike, and it will hurt more than a stick that's been loosely wrapped (step 6).

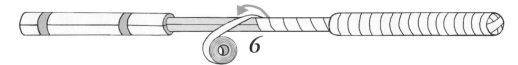

Inspect the weapon carefully to be sure that the entire length is adequately padded and that it has no rough edges that might cause abrasions (step 7).

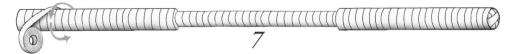

Your finished product should look something like this.

Finally, test it with your partner. Hit softly at first and gradually work up to harder and harder blows so you and your sparring partner can both get a feel for how hard you can fight safely with your particular weapons.

Understanding Timing

When it comes to combat, timing is a very important concept to study and understand. The Japanese martial arts distinguish three types of timing: *go no sen, sen no sen,* and *sen sen no sen.* The word *sen* means "initiative." These terms are useful to us in understanding how to control and win a fight.

Go no sen is the most basic timing. It means to counterattack after your response to the initial attack. For example, your opponent swings at you, and in response you block or evade, then strike back. First, there was the attack, followed by your response an instant later. There was a small delay between the two. This simple timing is most commonly employed by beginning students of staff fighting.

Sen no sen is an intermediate timing method and involves a simultaneous response to an incoming attack. In sen no sen, when you are attacked, you counter at the same time. There is no gap, no delay. The disarming blocks taught at levels 2 and 4 are good examples of tactics that utilize sen no sen timing; you target the opponent's lead hand with your block . . . or is it a strike?

Sen sen no sen timing refers to a preemptive movement or technique. Your opponent intends to launch an attack, but you prevent it before it can even take form. This is the most advanced form of timing, representing the highest state of awareness and control because it is the act of reading the opponent's intentions and knowing what they are going to do, almost before they do. It is a level of competency and understanding that only comes with years of diligent training.

So, say your opponent somehow gets the jump on you, swinging his staff downward intending to crack your skull. You barely have time to throw up a roof block to stop his attack before sharply sliding your staff down and into the opponent's lead hand. This is a good example of go no sen. The opponent pulls back to strike at you again. You are not surprised to see he has unconsciously chosen the most common habitual method of attack, a downward diagonal strike aimed at your head. You instantly plot the trajectory of his attack and initiate your own attack, intercepting the opponent's front hand midswing. This is a good example of sen no sen. Finally, your frustrated opponent moves to make a third swing, but before he can even initiate his attack, you attack his front thigh with a quick thrust strike. This thrust straightens his front knee and kills his momentum by preventing him from shifting his weight into the attack, stopping it before it even begins. This is sen sen no sen.

The Three-Step Rule

Drawing is a strategy, common to Western boxing, in which you purposely leave an opening in an attempt to get your opponent to attack you. While this may seem counterintuitive, it can be useful to create an opening for you to counterattack, and, since you are expecting the attack, you will be prepared to evade or defend. The Three-Step Rule can help you create effective drawing skills by developing a variety of tactics based on sound strategy.

1. Leave an opening your opponent *cannot* resist.
2. Wait until he is committed to the attack.
3. Counter where you know he will be open.

For example, since a right-to-left diagonal strike is one of the usual methods of attack, there is a very good chance that you can draw a right high strike by leaving your head exposed. The opponent will strike fast and hard when he takes the bait, and he may take it the instant it is offered, so don't get caught sleeping! Be prepared to put up a wall block the instant your opponent moves to strike. Immediately hook-strike the opponent's hand and attempt to strip it, leading directly into a counterstrike with the other end of your staff. Immediately hook-strike again with the end that just struck in an attempt to completely disarm the attacker. Remember to continue counterstriking until the attacker is totally neutralized.

Learn to use the Three-Step Rule to subtly set up your opponents. The key is hours of slow practice with a partner. Leave openings and have your partner attack as he would in combat but at half speed. React and counterattack at half speed as well. Moving slowly allows you to concentrate on refining your techniques as opposed to moving quickly and instinctively, which does not allow for analysis and evaluation during the execution, when the most progress and improvement take place. Use this time to learn how to see, feel, and flow. Speed will come later of its own accord and, when it does, your techniques will flow quickly without the appearance of being hurried or rushed.

Teaching staff fighting at Cuong Nhu's International Annual Training Camp in 2009.

Programming

The human mind can be very predictable. We know that our brains have a natural tendency to look for patterns, and we can use this knowledge to trick our opponents into doing what we want them to do. This is called **programming.** Programming is an exceptional method of setting up your techniques so as to maximize your probability of eluding your opponent's defenses in order to land a decisive, disabling strike.

To begin, deliver a strike to any open target. If it is blocked, retreat to your ready position, only to attack the same target again in the same manner a moment later. Each time, observe how your opponent counters your technique and quickly determine where he is open in that instant. The third time you attack, your opponent will subconsciously expect the same attack you have thrown previously. Use that expectation to your advantage by feinting with the initial technique before striking where your opponent has left himself open. Again, timing is important. Do not strike on a 1–2 practice count, as it allows the opponent an opportunity to adjust and counter your technique. Instead, strike on the half-beat . . . not 1–2, but 1–1.5!

Although this example demonstrates the concept of programming using three repetitions of the same technique, you may be able to draw an appropriate response using only two repetitions.

Programming: Your opponent's head seems open, but your initial attack is blocked, so you retreat.

Throw an identical technique, observing his reaction before quickly retreating.

Begin the same, but this time feint, abruptly changing the direction of your attack.

Continuation of Attack

Once you have committed to an attack, it is inefficient to pull back and reset to launch a second attack should your first attack fail. It takes too long to retract your weapon because the motion leaves an opportunity for your opponent to go on the offensive. It is usually more effective to press your attack, attempting a second strike without retracting your weapon. Western fencing calls this concept "continuation of attack," while wing chun gongfu refers to it as "the theory of advancement."

If you miss your target, you are basically left with three choices: (1) retract and reset before attacking again, which we have just mentioned takes time and leaves an opening for your opponent to launch a counterattack; (2) arc into a second strike; or (3) cut back by reversing the direction of your weapon, striking from the direction opposite to your original strike without retracting the staff.

When arcing into a second strike, it is important to keep your staff moving, preserving what momentum you can, in order to add it to your next strike. Try to reorient and launch a new attack, striking a target on the side opposite your original attack. If you are unable to recalibrate quickly enough, or if no target is readily available to you on the opposite side, continue the motion a full 360 degrees, returning to the side of your original attack, although probably not to the original line of attack since new opportunities will likely present themselves. This is also a good technique to use against a parry.

Continuation: Begin from a middle-grip ready position.

Deliver a basic number-1 strike, which the opponent evades by ducking.

Rather than retracting the tip to strike again, continue the motion of your strike, arcing back toward the opponent.

Strike to the first available target, in this case behind the lead knee. You can finish with a heel strike to the neck (inset).

You can also cut back to attack the same target from the opposite side. You will need to decelerate quickly in order to reverse the direction of your staff as soon as you realize you will or have missed the target. Cut back quickly and penetrate deeper toward the target in order to catch the opponent while he is still exposed.

A clever strategy to use, especially against a strong blocker, is to *purposely* miss on your first strike, narrowly bypassing the resulting block in order to quickly take the opposing line. Since this was your intended action all along, you can begin reversing your motion very quickly, cutting back deeply enough to impact the target on the side opposite your original swing.

The Cut Back: Begin in a middle-grip ready position.

Deliver a number-1 strike to draw a standard block. As you are about to make contact, retract the tip just enough that your strike bypasses the block.

Immediately cut back, leaning forward to close the gap enough to strike the target.

Finally, you can apply the strategy of continuation to pursue other avenues of attack even after your staff has been intercepted, blocked, or otherwise brought to a standstill. By not overcommitting to your first attack, you can react quickly, arcing into another open line of attack. If you anticipate the block, you may even be able to harness the resulting momentum from the impact with the opponent's staff to begin powering your next attack.

Redirection: Start from a standard guard.

Open with a number-5 vertical downward strike, which the opponent moves to block.

Seeing that you are going to be blocked, immediately redirect your strike to another available target, in this case the midsection.

Blitz Attacks

Closing the gap between you and your opponent to land a strike without getting hit yourself is one of the trickiest parts of fighting with the staff. We have already covered the basic footwork patterns, but there are some special methods for closing the gap with utmost speed and surprise. These are the blitz attacks.

Leaping

Leaping entails jumping forward suddenly with both feet at the same time. The idea is to cover a lot of ground very quickly, not to jump high. Attempt to skim the ground with your feet as you leap forward and attack. Your strike should land just as you do. Do not make the mistake of leaping and then attacking; to time it correctly you need to initiate both movements simultaneously.

Leaping: Begin holding your staff in middle grip and standing just outside of striking range, putting your opponent at ease since she thinks you cannot reach her.

Without making any telegraphing motions, suddenly leap forward, pushing off with both feet, and initiate a right-to-left strike with the tip of your staff.

As you land, strike the opponent's head with a sharp, focused strike. Impact the target an instant before your front foot hits the ground in order to transfer the greatest possible amount of momentum into your strike.

Flèche

This blitz move is adapted from a Western fencing technique called the *flèche*. Flèche is French for "arrow." You should feel like an arrow shot from a powerful bow. The idea is to keep from telegraphing your movement until it is already well under way.

Begin with a smooth but rapid transfer of all your weight onto your front foot, then push off on the ball of that foot as you quickly step your rear foot ahead to catch yourself. Though the move is initiated by your rear foot, it is the ball of your front foot that provides the explosive forward momentum for the technique. You should land your strike on the opponent just before your rear foot lands. Your momentum should carry you past your opponent to the side, hopefully limiting his opportunity to launch a counterattack. If you can recover before your opponent, your new position may offer you an opportunity to launch an unexpected attack from a new angle.

Flèche: Begin holding your staff in middle grip and standing just outside of striking range.

Shift your weight to your right foot as you begin leaning toward the opponent, keeping your staff still to prevent telegraphing your intention.

As you begin to fall forward, drive explosively off your lead foot, striking to the opponent's head with the tip of your staff, drawing an appropriate block. You should stay committed to the technique so that if the opponent does not block, you can strike her effectively.

As you continue falling forward, you will need to step through with your rear foot to catch yourself. As you do, begin a left horizontal heel strike.

Impact the target an instant before your front foot hits the ground, transferring the greatest possible amount of momentum into the strike.

Let your forward momentum carry you past the opponent, making it very difficult, if not impossible, for her to launch a counterattack.

The Grand Overall Strategy

When confronting an opponent, it is advisable to begin with a sound overall strategy that has been tested and proven effective in combat. While everyone is encouraged to develop an overall strategy (actually, a set of different strategies with corresponding tactics) based on what works best for him or her, I have found that the following overall strategy, when applied aggressively, works well against most opponents.

The Grand Overall Strategy is best learned in full-speed, full-contact matches, where either the participants are armored or the weapons are padded, or both. The ultimate goal is to train to make sure your strategy (the overall plan and goal) and tactics (the specific techniques you will use to implement that plan and achieve that goal) will work well in actual combat. The Grand Strategy is a simple (easy to remember) and general (easy to apply) two-phase roadmap to victory.

Begin the opening phase of the fight in extended grip. Stay out of range of your opponent's strikes while feeling the opponent out by continually striking to the closest available targets (usually the hands and front knee or ankle) the instant he crosses into your range (the circle of death). Remember that you should avoid taking any hits and that this feeling-out period will probably not last very long. You must be ready to jump into phase 2 at any moment.

Phase 2 begins when your opponent realizes that he is taking damage while not delivering any. The smarter your opponent is, the quicker he will realize the secret to your success: the extended grip. Usually the opponent will then try to adopt the extended grip himself to level the playing field. But victory comes easiest on an uneven field, so while you may engage in extended-grip combat for a few more moves, at the earliest opportunity you should pass the end of the opponent's staff with a wall block or parry, close range suddenly, and shift to middle grip, striking repeatedly with both ends of your staff. Since your strikes flow quickly from both sides (indeed, from all angles), the opponent will be momentarily overcome while he struggles to block or counter in the much less effective extended grip. This is an excellent opportunity to attempt a partial or complete disarm using the hooking double strikes.

As soon as the opponent mounts a solid defense, and especially if he should shift back to middle grip, you should immediately disengage, retreating on an angle as you shift back to extended grip. Don't drop straight back, or you may become the victim. It is important that you cover your retreat by dropping some long, sharp strikes on the opponent to prevent him from locking back onto you, all the while looking for the best angle and target for your next attack.

Take care not to let your opponent do to you what you did to him. Control the fight by keeping your opponent at extended range until you see the need to wade in with middle grip again, usually just after the opponent has had the bright idea that he might do better going back to extended grip.

In this manner, it is possible to stay one step ahead of the opponent. As long as the opponent keeps chasing your lead, you should be able to dominate the fight, as he will be caught in a loop of trying to reorient himself and, therefore, unable to mount an effective strategy of his own.

Remember that the Grand Overall Strategy is used in conjunction with everything you have already learned, including feints, combinations, programming, double strikes, hand strikes, hooking disarms, and every other technique in your arsenal, as you switch between ranges and grips to outwit and ultimately defeat your opponent.

Your ultimate goal must be the seamless integration of all the various techniques at your disposal, applied in such a way that your opponent gets hit while you do not.

Live Steel Fight Academy's 2005 Tournament, where I took home Grand Champion after a hard day of fighting. I won five out of eight events that day: long sword, dagger, rapier and dagger, submission grappling, and, of course, staff.

The Seven Principal Rules

The Schoole of the Noble and Worthy Science of Defence was written in 1617 by English fencing master Joseph Swetnam. In it he lays out his *"seven principal rules where on true defence is grounded."* Even in modern times, these rules still make up the foundation of almost every martial art. You would do well to learn them.

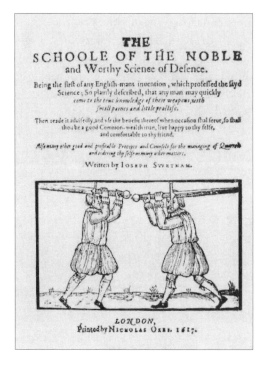

1. **A Good Guard:** . . . when thou hast thy guard it is not enough to know it, but to keep it so long as thou art within reach or danger of thy enemie.

2. **True Observing of Distance:** . . . thou shouldest stand so far of from thine enemy, as thou canst, but reach him when thou dost step forth with thy blow or thrust. . . .

3. **To Know the Place:** . . . thou must marke which is the nearest part of thine enemie towards thee, and which lieth most unregarded, whether it be his . . . hand, his knee, or his leg, or where thous maist best hurt him at a large distance without danger to thy selfe.

4. **To Take Time:** . . . when opportunity is proffered thee, . . . then make a quicke answer . . . quicker than I can speake it. . . .

5. **To Keep Space:** . . . if thou charge thy enemy . . . recover thy weapons into their place, and draw thy selfe into thy guard againe, and so preparing thy selfe for to defend, and likewise to make a fresh assault with discretion. . . .

6. **Patience:** . . . is one of the greatest virtues that can be in a man: the Wise man saith, he is a foole which cannot governe himself. . . .

7. **Often Practice:** . . . without practice the Proverbe says, a man may forget his *Pater noster.** . . . For skill to everie reasonable man is a friend . . . by which meanes such have great advantage of the ignorant and unskillful. . . .

*Pater noster is Latin for "Our Father," a prayer so prevalent in Swetnam's society that it was unthinkable that anyone could ever forget it.

Level-6 Workout

Objective: To learn how to apply your staff-fighting skills against an opponent.

1. Warm-Up: Five to ten minutes. Do some slow shadow sparring against an imaginary opponent. Move slowly at first. Picture your opponent, visualizing his movements as you react, attacking and defending. As your mind and body warm up, gradually increase your speed, but do not go so hard that you get tired or out of breath.

2. Distancing/Control: Ten to fifteen minutes. Even though this is a control drill, it is recommended that you wear protective gear on your head, hands, elbows, and knees. Use light rattan or even padded staves. Begin by facing your opponent and *slowly* moving around just outside your opponent's striking range. Observe your opponent's stance and movements. When you see an opening and sense the opportunity to attack, strike to the target but *do not* make contact. Stop the action, reset, and repeat. This drill should be performed at half speed, gradually increasing in tempo only after both practitioners have become proficient at controlling their strikes.

3. Accuracy/Timing: Ten to fifteen minutes. As mentioned above, after a while, both partners will begin speeding up, making it harder and harder to control your strikes. This is the natural evolution of the drill, but should be postponed as long as possible. When you do start inadvertently hitting each other, it is time to switch to phase 2. Even though you are free fighting, both partners need to continue to exercise control. Let each exchange run its course, then break and reset. Concentrate on fast, accurate shots that hit while not allowing your opponent to hit you in return. Be mindful and move with purpose. Your mission is to methodically test each technique in your arsenal, figuring out what works when and why.

4. Power: Ten to fifteen minutes. Take a few minutes to test some of your newfound techniques on the heavy bag, striking post, tire, or other sort of pell. Aside from developing power, working alone with a piece of equipment allows you the opportunity after sparring to physically review and mentally catalogue the techniques that worked for you so they will be retained in your mind and muscles for future reference and use.

5. Cool Down: Five to ten minutes. It is important to take some time at the end of your workout to do some light stretching. This will help your muscles stay loose and recover faster. Faster recovery time means you will feel better and can get back to training again that much sooner.

Key phrase for this workout:
Don't fight hard, fight smart.

Hot Stuff

Level 7 consists of techniques that I like to call *"hot stuff."* These techniques don't fit neatly into the sections on basic fighting skills and are not necessary to a basic understanding of staff combat. But they are crucial if you are to become an expert on staff fighting. In this level, you will learn special techniques and deceptive tricks that will enable you to defeat bigger, stronger, and faster opponents. These techniques require knowledge and skill to execute effectively. That is why I am presenting them *in addition* to the core curriculum. A beginner would find them almost useless without having first mastered the skills in levels 1–6.

Switching Grips

Up to now we have predominately used a standard right-handed grip. However, it can be advantageous to be ambidextrous with the staff and able to adopt a left-leading middle or extended grip with the same comfort and ease as the right. Changing your lead in the midst of combat can momentarily throw off your opponent, giving you an opportunity to attack before he can reorient to your new position.

Switching leads must be done quickly and smoothly to preserve the element of surprise in order to prevent your opponent from countering. From a standard right grip, begin the motion by sliding your rear hand to the base of your lead hand, then quickly slip your lead hand back to take the place of the rear hand. Switch foot positions simultaneously to lead with your opposite foot. With practice, you should be able to change from a right guard to a left guard in one fluid motion and launch directly into an unexpected attack.

It is not enough to merely know how to switch grips. You must relearn everything you have learned on your nondominant side so you can execute the techniques with equal proficiency with either hand leading. Whenever your opponent thinks he has the upper hand, you have the option to switch grips on him. It will keep your opponent guessing, as he will need time to observe your change in position, *reorient* himself, decide on a new course of action, and then act—the famous "OODA Loop" (observe, orient, decide, act) developed by military strategist USAF Colonel John Boyd. If you are not familiar with this concept, you would be wise to look it up. While it may take the opponent only a second to go through this process, that should provide you with sufficient opportunity to launch an attack, catching your opponent both mentally and physically unprepared.

Alternate Ready Positions

We have mainly worked from two guarding positions: the basic middle grip and the basic extended-grip ready positions. While these are essential standard guards, they are not the only ones available to you. The following ready positions are not designed to offer you protection. Instead, they are well-laid traps that rely on deception, earning them the name "trick guards." Instead of starting from one of these positions, allowing your opponent the opportunity to study your position and figure out your plan, it is better to adopt an alternate ready position suddenly in the midst of combat. In the heat of the moment, your opponent is far more likely to get greedy and take the bait.

Fool's Guard

One of the most deceptive ready positions is the fool's guard, so named because it leaves your entire body seemingly exposed to attack; but, as the saying goes, only fools rush in. In reality, the tip of your staff is closer to your opponent in this guard than in any other, and a mere raising of the tip or pushing down on the heel lifts the tip of your staff into the opponent as he attacks. Once the opponent begins stepping forward, he is committed to moving in that direction until he can replant his foot. If your timing is good, you can catch him midstride and hit him square in the face or throat, killing his momentum and disrupting his attack.

Fool's Guard: Start from a back stance in extended grip, with the tip of your staff held low, but not touching the ground, because it would be slower to raise your weapon from a resting position. You must be deceptive, and make your opponent believe that you are open to his attack. Be patient and let him make the first move.

Watch your opponent's feet with your peripheral vision. Once drawn into attacking you, he will have to initiate his movement with a step. Immediately shift into a forward stance, raising the tip of your staff into the path of his body, snapping your rear hip forward. Target the throat, letting the opponent skewer himself on the tip of your staff.

Tail Guard

The tail guard is assumed by dropping the tip of your staff down and behind you. This position appears to leave you defenseless; however, as in each of the trick guards, this is seldom the case so long as you have good timing and are able to control the distance. Be ready to step forward with your rear foot to close the gap, or quickly step back with your front foot to maintain proper distancing should the opponent rush you. Both maneuvers place you in a strong position to effectively attack your opponent's ankle, knee, groin, or ribs.

A tail guard can set up attacks to a variety of targets. knee (1), ribs (2), lead arm (3), or head (4).

High Guard

The high guard looks like you are just standing there with the staff resting on your shoulder. You appear open and defenseless, and you are . . . as open and defenseless as a bear trap. Lead with your left foot as you stand just out of range of your opponent. Hold your staff in extended grip, right hand on top, and place it over your right shoulder. The idea is to look so relaxed as to invite an overt attack. Let the tip of your staff droop to about a 45-degree angle, but not much farther, as it will take you too long to bring your staff into play once the opponent decides to launch his attack.

If the opponent approaches cautiously, you can advance on him by stepping forward with your right foot to close the gap unexpectedly as you strike vertically downward with the tip of the staff.

If the opponent rushes in to close the gap, retreat by stepping backward with your left foot into a right stance, giving just enough ground to maintain proper distancing for a focused strike with the tip of your staff.

High Guard: Starting from the high guard (1), as your opponent advances, drop your front foot back and begin the strike (2). Keep the staff in contact with your shoulder for as long as possible as you execute the strike (3). You will need to follow up immediately after the strike. One option is to switch directions (4) and deliver a straight thrust to the opponent's throat (5).

While training with some friends in the SCA (Society for Creative Anachronism), I once fought a sixteen-year-old kid who wore minimal armor and wielded the most ridiculous sword I had ever seen. It was made from thick rattan, as all our weapons were, but it was over six feet long with a two-foot cross guard. At the time I could not take him seriously; he just stood there before me with that stupid sword slung over his shoulder. I was sure I was going to tear this kid up.

I was thinking that someone should have rung a school bell, because class was about to be called to session. The only thing is, I didn't realize that *I* was the one who was about to get schooled!

First I found out why he wore so little armor: I couldn't get close enough to hit him. Every time I tried to close the gap with my normal-length long sword, the kid would fall back and drop a brutally hard strike on me. It was so fast that the first few rang off my helmet before I could get up an effective block; then he started targeting my hands. I have a really nice pair of steel clamshell gauntlets, but after only a few strikes I could hardly hold my sword and had to yield the fight.

Whenever I get my butt kicked, I like to analyze *why*. Then I get practicing. I figure that if a technique is good enough to beat me, then it will probably work on most others. I study my opponent's technique, come to understand it, then I work hard to steal it and add it to my arsenal.

The key to the high guard is a powerful shoulder lever driven by the movement of your entire body, either forward or backward. As you move, bend your torso forward, dipping your shoulder into the strike in order to keep the shaft of the staff in contact with your shoulder for as long as possible. With good footwork and timing you should be able to drop bombs on your opponent, preventing him from ever crossing the gap.

Begin in the high guard.

Hold your position until your opponent is committed to moving forward.

Then spring the trap. Step back as you deliver a downward strike to the lead hand.

Stop your strike as soon as it is complete.

Take advantage of the open line and thrust to the throat.

To ensure full penetration of the target, be sure to finish the thrust in a full lunge.

The shoulder lever can also be used in conjunction with the hanging guard that you learned in the Donga drill (see level 4). To practice the shoulder lever you can use a modified version of the Donga drill, anchoring the staff to your shoulder just before you deliver the strike. You can also try applying the levering concept to a horizontal strike, driving forward using your upper arm as the fulcrum, as opposed to the shoulder.

Rear Guard

Take a look at this picture of young quarterstaff fighters from the late 1800s. The boy on the left has adopted a basic extended grip, while his opponent on the right is holding his staff in a rear guard. As you can probably see, the rear guard is another trick guard. While appearing to be open and defenseless, he is actually goading his opponent into stepping into range. When he does, the boy in rear guard has the option of delivering a powerful downward extended strike from the right (possibly incorporating the shoulder lever as previously discussed under high guard) or an upward extended diagonal strike from the left.

Proper application of the rear guard depends on controlling the distance between you and your opponent. As with the high guard, be ready to step back quickly if the opponent charges to close the gap, staying out of range while maintaining the distance you need to land an effective strike with the tip of your staff.

Top Down: Adopt a right rear guard.

As the opponent begins to close, pivot to your left, feinting a left upward diagonal strike and drawing an expected response.

Quickly reverse directions, twisting to your right, as you switch to extended grip.

Use a shoulder lever to strike the lead hand.

If the opponent is hovering at the edge of your range, reluctant to step in, you can take a chance and step forward to close the gap, striking either downward from above or upward from below.

The rear guard is especially deceptive because the strike can come from either side, making it three-dimensional, as compared to the other trick guards that can only strike from one side. You can feint by making a small motion in one direction to draw your opponent into defending that area, only to strike swiftly from the opposite side. However, as with all the trick guards, you are choosing to adopt an inherently weak position, leaving you purposely exposed to attack. Be careful not to overuse these guards, or you may find yourself the one being lured into a trap!

Bottom Up: Begin in a right rear guard.

Feint a right strike, drawing the opponent's attention to your right side, as you subtly slide to a left extended grip.

Quickly switch directions, twisting to your left as you release your right hand.

Strike to the opponent's right side, hitting to the head, elbow, ribs, knee, or ankle.

A more dynamic approach to the rear guard can be seen in a combination called the uppercut-chop that I borrowed from Shaolin gongfu. The idea is to quickly flow through the rear guard directly into an offensive technique. While the technique demonstrated is the classic uppercut-chop, the same load-up can just as easily lead into other strikes such as a devastating horizontal knee strike.

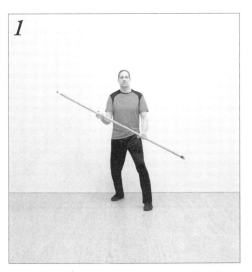

Uppercut-Chop: Drop your guard to draw a high strike.

As the opponent moves to attack, sweep upward to block his strike.

Flow through the block, dropping the staff behind your back as you step forward with your right foot.

Momentarily release the staff with your left hand so you can swing it through with your right and re-grab it with your left hand.

Continue striking in an upward arc.

At the top of the swing, use your shoulder to quickly return the staff as you step forward with your left foot.

Finish with a downward strike, just as we did from the high guard.

Additional Techniques

Like the alternate guards, these additional techniques can bring variety to your arsenal. They are meant to complement the core curriculum. Use them sparingly. As the old adage warns, go to the well once too often, and the bottom will eventually fall out of your bucket.

Upward Heel Strike

From a basic middle-grip ready position, leading with your right foot, you can deliver a quick stationary upward vertical heel strike, or step forward with your left foot to close the distance between you and your opponent as you drive upward with the heel of the staff.

This strike is different from strike number 6, the upward vertical strike from the nine basic strikes (see level 1), because the power hand is on the same side of your body. Since the power hand is not crossing your body, you can transfer the energy of your rear hip and leg directly into the strike, resulting in a far more powerful blow.

Applying the principle of continuation of attack, the upward heel strike can lead into an overhand heel thrust (see next technique). The upward heel strike is also useful as part of a high disarming beat (covered later in this chapter).

The upward heel strike (left). Notice the distance covered when combined with a step (right).

Overhand Heel Thrust

The overhand heel thrust is a powerful, close-range attack delivered from either the middle or extended-grip position. In this technique, your staff is first raised high over your shoulder, with the tip pointing behind you, allowing you to drive the butt of the staff firmly into your target. As with all thrusting techniques, pull your strike back quickly and reset, ready to defend or attack again. A heel thrust can stop a man in his tracks.

A full-power overhand heel thrust in full armor! (Photo by Roland Warzecha)

The overhand heel thrust relies on good timing and sure footwork to land successfully. If the opponent is charging you, the technique can be performed stationary, using the opponent's forward momentum to impale him on your staff.

The problem with this strike is that it starts from a high position with the staff held mostly behind you, leaving you exposed to a quick attack, especially along the lower line. Therefore, the overhand thrust is often best when combined with good footwork to close the gap. The chambering motion can appear to your opponent as an upward strike, serving to confuse his defense and setting you up for a successful thrust. The overhand heel thrust also works well as a quick follow-up to an upward heel strike, horizontal heel strike, or high beat disarm (see level 7).

Overhand Heel Thrust: Begin with a middle grip.

Raise your staff overhead.

Rather than completely stopping the staff and starting from a standstill, keep the weapon moving in a tight arc to maintain some momentum as you reverse the direction of the staff and thrust forward and downward into the target.

Jabbing Thrusts

As we learned in level 4, fixed-hand thrusts are very strong, while slip thrusts are weaker. There is a third type of thrust, the one-handed jabbing thrust. While it is usually not as forceful as the other two strikes, it offers a little more range and a different angle of attack. Jabbing thrusts can be delivered from the middle or extended grip.

Begin by pointing the tip of your staff at your intended target. Drive the staff forward with your rear hand, releasing your lead hand momentarily. Allow the rear arm to fully extend and drive the tip directly into

An overhand jabbing thrust from the side.

your target. Good targets include the face, throat, solar plexus, and groin. Pull the staff back immediately and catch it in your lead hand, ready to defend or attack again.

To add force to your jabbing thrust, step forward as you strike. This closes the gap quickly, adding to the surprise of your jabbing thrust.

Jabbing Thrust: Begin from a standard extended grip in back stance, standing just out of range for a slip thrust, giving the opponent the illusion of safety.

Shift into forward stance, releasing your grip on the weapon with your left hand as you thrust the staff forward with your right arm, delivering an underhanded jabbing thrust. Twist your hip sharply into the technique for maximum force on the strike. Since this type of single-handed thrust is not very powerful (even with the hip rotation), it is usually only effective against very sensitive targets such as the groin, throat, or face.

Poisonous Snake Coming Out from the Cave

This is a Chinese technique I learned from *The Ferocious Enchanted Staff of the Ancient Monks*, by Master Monk Yuan Wan. As a teenager, legendary wing chun instructor Leung Ting originally purchased a copy of this old manual from a used book stall on the streets of Hong Kong and had it reprinted.

Opponents often have a tendency to target your head, especially if you purposely leave it open in order to draw

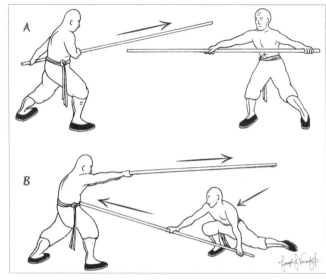

(Author's re-creation)

an attack using the Three-Step Rule (see level 6). "Poisonous Snake Coming Out from the Cave" (the Chinese love elaborate names) entails evading the incoming head strike by waiting until the opponent is committed to his high-line attack, then suddenly dropping below his weapon to attack from the low line with a slip thrust or jabbing thrust. Good targets include the groin, solar plexus, and throat. This technique may require more practice than most. It takes considerable flexibility to drop into a very low lunging stance and strong leg muscles to rise up out of it quickly and smoothly enough to effectively defend or press your attack.

Poisonous Snake Coming Out from the Cave: Using the Three-Step Rule as a guide, leave your head open to draw a high strike from your opponent.

When the attack comes, be ready to drop below the level of the strike.

Use a slip thrust to poke your opponent in the throat.

Follow through by twisting your hip into the strike as you forcefully straighten your rear arm.

Fiore's Block

Occasionally, you may need to defend yourself with only one hand on the staff. Since a good block needs to be anchored on two spots along the staff, you can place the heel against the ground to anchor it.

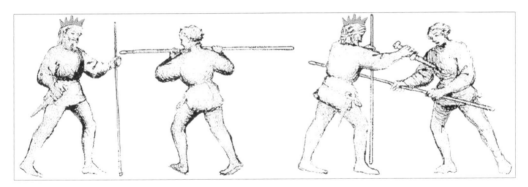

Illustrations from Fiore's *Flower of Battle*, 1410.

This essentially gives you a one-handed wall block. To defend, simply stay on the side of the wall opposite the opponent's attack. This technique is made easier by slightly moving the staff from side to side using your top hand.

This move is named for Italian fencing master Fiore dei Liberi, as it first appears in his 1410 combat treatise *Flower of Battle* (*Fior di Battaglia*). Fiore used the staff in conjunction with a dagger or sword, blocking to one side while stabbing to the other.

Lacking a second weapon, Fiore's block frees one of your hands so that you may effectively check the opponent's weapon as you simultaneously grasp his staff. Dropping your own staff allows you to close the gap and disarm the opponent.

Fiore's Block: From a middle guard, leave your head open to draw a strike.

As the opponent takes the bait, plant the heel of your staff on the ground and block the strike.

Enter immediately with a single step.

Drop your own staff in order to grasp the opponent's staff firmly with both hands.

Begin turning counterclockwise as you step in.

Disarm the opponent with a strong twist of your body.

Disarming Beat

A normal beat (see level 5) is designed to clear a line of attack, but the aim of the disarming beat is to strike your opponent's weapon with the intent of knocking it partially or completely from his grip. The most important aspect of this technique is to strike from the proper angle. The staff can only be forced out of your opponent's hand through the gap between his thumb and forefinger. Striking at the proper angle is key, as striking the staff into the opponent's palm will not result in a release of the weapon.

In staff fighting, as in all combat arts, it is important to read the opponent and apply the proper technique at the proper time in order to get your desired result. Observe how your opponent is holding his weapon. If you notice he is keeping a loose grip on his staff, this is the perfect time to apply a disarming beat. Using this technique against an opponent who is gripping his staff tightly, your chances of disarming him will be greatly reduced.

There is a way to help loosen even the tightest of grips, however. Hand strikes have the potential to greatly diminish your opponent's grip strength.

Overhead Disarming Beat: Face off in a middle grip.

Feint a vertical downward strike to the opponent's head in order to draw an overhead block.

As the opponent commits to the block, quickly reverse directions, striking upward with the heel and knocking the weapon from her hands.

Follow up immediately with an overhand thrust.

Trapping and Pinning

One of the best ways to keep from getting hit is to control the opponent's weapon. As we've seen, this can be achieved through the effective use of blocks and parries. To enhance this skill set, we are going to add trapping and pinning principles to immobilize the opponent's weapon momentarily, giving your counterattack the maximum chance of success.

Trapping entails immobilizing the opponent's weapon. You can trap an opponent's weapon by grabbing it with your hand or by hooking your arm around it. You can also trap the opponent's weapon by pressing it against his own body, preventing him from striking you. Pinning is when you use the ground to restrict the movement of the opponent's weapon. You can pin the opponent's staff with your own staff by pressing it into the ground (see below). You can also use your leg to step or kneel on the opponent's staff. The tremendous downward pressure exerted on his weapon by your leg can either drag him to the ground or strip the staff from his grasp.

The Carry Over: The opponent strikes from right to left, which you block.

Use the opponent's momentum against him, immediately stepping through with your rear foot and beating the opponent's staff downward.

Continue through with your beat, pinning the opponent's staff to the ground momentarily.

Quickly reverse directions, striking along the open upper line.

Flying Front Kick

The flying front kick is a special type of blitz attack. The idea is to close the gap with a long step as you parry the opponent's staff upward, clearing the low line for a sudden unexpected kicking attack. As with all blitz attacks, you will need to move forward suddenly without telegraphing your intentions. It is also important that your opponent be focused on striking you with the tip of his weapon at the moment you blitz. An opponent who reads your intention, or who is not committed to a strike with the tip, can counter with a low-line attack, such as an upward heel strike to your groin, as you are sailing forward through the air.

Flying Front Kick: One way to ensure your opponent is focusing on striking you with the tip of her weapon is to leave your head open purposely.

Once you perceive the opponent's attention has momentarily shifted to this exposed target, explode forward! Lift your front foot as you push forward off your rear foot to close the gap, raising your staff overhead to block perpendicular to the opponent's staff.

Swing your rear foot forward.

Drive the knee upward as you leap into the air.

At the top of your jump, switch your feet.

Drive the lead leg forward into your opponent's stomach or groin. Strike to the stomach, striking with the ball of your foot, flexing your toes up and back toward your shin. Attack the groin by striking upward from underneath, impacting with the instep of your foot. Smash the testicles of a male opponent against his body. Groin attacks are also effective against women.

Flicking

Staff combat is often practiced in a large, open space with floors clear of obstructions. Since serious combat would likely take place in a natural environment, indoors or out, it is important to learn how to use the given environment to our greatest advantage. With proper training, you will not only get used to having objects and obstacles all around you, you will also learn to use this helpful clutter to befuddle and defeat your opponent.

Flicking is a technique in which you use your staff to propel an item at your opponent. This was a technique made famous by the fishermen of Okinawa, who practiced self-defense with the *eku*, or oar. Imagine a fisherman bringing in the day's haul when some local hoodlums decide they are going to take it away from him. The fisherman grabs the nearest weapon, an oar. As the thugs approach him, he flicks sand into their eyes with the wide blade. His blinded opponents receive some quick, sharp blows before they wisely decide to retreat and run away.

Flicking is not limited to sand, sticks, and leaves. Imagine you stop in at the local tavern when a scuffle breaks out. Try as you might to avoid the situation, you find yourself confronted with several would-be attackers, so you grab the nearest convenient weapon, a pool cue. Instead of engaging immediately, however, you buy yourself some time and space by hooking the handle of a beer mug off the bar and flicking it into the face of your nearest opponent. Ouch!

Flicking: Your opponent stands out of range. He is not alarmed as you casually place the end of your staff on the ground. He may even take this as a sign that you have become complacent and have dropped your guard.

Without telegraphing your intention, suddenly flick the item directly into the opponent's face.

Immediately take advantage of the split-second opportunity you have created to close the gap and strike.

Throwing

There are times when you may find it tactically desirable to throw your staff at an opponent. The strength of the throw is in its extended range and the fact that it is usually an unexpected technique that can catch an opponent off guard. The obvious weakness is that, if you throw your staff, you are disarming yourself, so it is not a technique that should be used on a whim.

Throwing is sometimes the only sound choice you have, especially if your opponent has a projectile weapon, such as a throwing knife or a gun. If you can't reach the opponent with your staff, but he can reach you, then your staff is useless as a handheld weapon. Therefore, do not become overly attached to it. A well-placed throw will force your opponent to either dodge or block your attack, which creates an opportunity, a momentary distraction, that you can exploit by immediately following up, either by fleeing the situation or by quickly closing the gap to disarm and otherwise neutralize the opponent.

It is important that you do not telegraph your intention by chambering for the throw too abruptly. Instead, draw the staff back as you casually shift your weight to your back foot to avoid alerting the opponent and setting off his alarms. Then throw sharply and strongly, getting your body mass behind your throw by transferring your weight to your front foot as you twist your hips into the throw. You can throw the staff either vertically or horizontally.

It is important to keep in mind that a vertical throw can be sidestepped, a high horizontal throw can be ducked under, and a very low horizontal throw could be jumped over, especially if you telegraph your move. Follow up immediately after the throw—do not hesitate for even an instant!

Throwing: Draw the staff back and shift your weight to your rear foot, preparing for the throw.

Shift your weight to your front foot and snap your hip forward as you release either vertically or horizontally.

LEVEL 8
Master Staff Training

Level 8 focuses on some very advanced aspects of staff training: close combat, ground work, facing multiple opponents, and unarmed defense against the staff. These activities can be very dangerous and they require the participants to have a good deal of skill with the staff; therefore, they are not recommended for novices.

Close Combat with the Staff

The staff can buy you a lot of space, but unfortunately you won't always have the luxury. You may find yourself in a confined space, or facing an opponent who has successfully closed the gap on you. In times like these, you will have to employ close-in levers, pushes, and pokes coupled with good footwork to get yourself out of any tight jams.

Close combat occurs when your opponent is within arm's or leg's reach. If you are in middle grip, you can punch out strongly with both hands, striking with the middle section of the staff. If you are caught in extended grip, you will want to strike and thrust with the butt end of the weapon. This is precisely why spears and pole arms were often equipped with a weighted, sometimes pointed, butt cap. These techniques are best practiced against a simple wooden striking post as, even without a butt cap, they have the potential to tear a heavy bag.

Striking with the Center Section of the Staff: Intercept the opponent's attack.

As you intercept, use the tip of your staff to parry the opponent's weapon in a counterclockwise motion, opening the opponent's high line to attack.

Step in as you raise the heel.

Strike forcefully to the opponent's neck with the center section of your staff.

Above all, always remember that your whole body can be used as a weapon. The staff is merely a power multiplier. Head butts, elbow strikes, knee strikes, and foot stomps are effective attacks when an opponent crowds too close or starts to grapple you. A strong thrusting front kick can push a close opponent back into an effective striking range for the staff. If your weapon gets tied up to the point that it becomes a disadvantage to you, it should be abandoned immediately in favor of empty-hand striking. You do not have to give the weapon up completely, however. If your opponent grabs or traps your weapon, let go with one hand just long enough to execute some effective strikes. Then re-grab your weapon. It should not be trapped as effectively as before.

Elbow Strike: You attempt an overhand heel thrust to the opponent's face.

The opponent parries your staff downward, pinning it to the ground.

The opponent now has a clear line of attack to your head, but before he can reverse the direction of his strike, step in with your rear foot while checking his staff using Fiore's block to deliver a surprise elbow strike to the opponent's neck or jaw.

Groin Kick: The opponent comes within kicking range.

Deliver a swift upward instep kick to the groin.

You can also use the ground to momentarily pin and immobilize your opponent's staff.

Pin into a Takedown: The opponent strikes from right to left, which you block.

Use the opponent's momentum against him by immediately stepping through with your rear foot and beating the opponent's staff downward with the heel on your staff.

Continue through with your beat, knocking the opponent's staff to the ground.

Step your lead foot forward, placing your thigh across the back of the opponent's thigh as you bring the heel of your staff across his chest.

Twist your hips and shoulders to your left to make the opponent fall over your front leg.

You can easily follow up with a thrust using the heel of the staff.

Levering is another useful skill for close combat with the staff. It entails planting one end of your staff behind your opponent's supporting leg, then lifting or pressing against the opponent's body to unbalance him, possibly knocking him to the ground. Levering can be especially helpful in maneuvering an opponent into or over an environmental obstacle, such as a rock or a log. Levers can also be used to move an opponent into the path of other opponents, creating an obstacle to slow or restrict their approach. To learn more about levering, be sure to read appendix I, "Fighting Physics: The Mechanics of the Staff."

The Lever: Your opponent places too much weight on his front leg. From this position, he lacks mobility, making him susceptible to a well-placed lever.

Recognizing this, step forward and jam the opponent's staff by thrusting the middle section of your staff toward his face, drawing a middle section block.

Immediately slide the heel of your staff down and inside the opponent's lead leg as you continue to jam his weapon.

Press forward, levering against the inside of the opponent's knee.

Step forward and complete the lever.

A well-placed lever can send an unsuspecting opponent to the floor.

This is only the beginning. These examples as presented—the elbow, the kick, take-down, and lever—demonstrate only one variation on larger principles. Many other viable variations using related techniques exist. For example, there are many ways to lever an opponent with your staff. Explore the overall concepts and learn to apply their underlying principles. In this way, you will develop a deeper knowledge of the staff that will serve you better than learning sets of overly specific techniques.

Groundwork

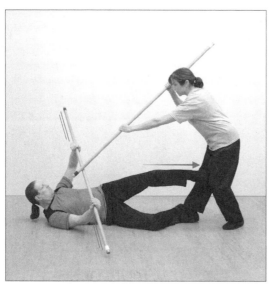

The Knee Press

Sooner or later, most fights go to the ground. Therefore, you need a good ground game. A strong foundation in a throwing art such as judo can help you throw your opponent offensively while defensively avoiding being thrown yourself. Good grappling skills help you on the ground, especially if you both end up there. Throwing and grappling are arts unto themselves and are outside the scope of this book. But I recommend learning and practicing them. This section concentrates mostly on the use of the staff *after* you have been knocked to the ground.

Whenever you find yourself on the ground, work to get back on your feet as soon as possible. Remember that you make an easy target while getting up, so it is sometimes strategically better to hold your position on the ground until you can get to your feet safely.

If you're on the ground, immediately roll to your back and spin to get your feet between you and your opponent. This puts your head, your most crucial target, farthest from the opponent's weapon and, perhaps more importantly, farthest from his feet so he can't kick you in the head. Keep your staff up and ready to block to either the left or the right sides.

Right block.

Center block.

Left block.

When you are standing, it is difficult to use your feet to protect you, but when you are on your back, your feet become very useful tools to block, kick, and trip. Thick-soled shoes, such as work boots, can provide good protection for your feet, acting as armor against your opponent's strikes. You can use your feet to redirect or even stop a staff strike. You can also kick or employ clever foot trips to bring the opponent down to your level.

Scissor Takedown: Control the opponent's approach by checking her lead knee with your left foot.

As she thrusts for your face, parry her strike to your left with the middle of your staff.

Switch your feet, hooking in front of her shin with your left instep as you roll onto your left side.

Hack down onto the opponent's calf with your right heel.

As you roll onto your back, bring her to her knees.

Use your momentum to continue rolling toward the opponent, momentarily immobilizing her by locking her right leg as you deliver a strike to the base of the skull.

Remember, you can still strike effectively with your staff from the ground.

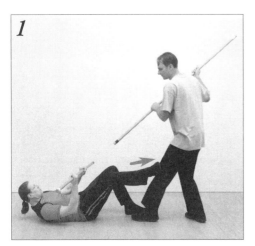

Kick/Strike Combination 1: The opponent has knocked you to the ground. Employ the Three-Step Rule, drawing the opponent in by seeming to leave yourself open to an easy finish.

As the opponent thrusts at you, swing your foot up and across your centerline, pressing his staff to the side.

Let the momentum from the leg technique lead your rotation into a strike to the opponent's neck with the tip of your staff.

Kick/Strike Combination 2: Use your feet and staff together in logical combinations to defend, open lines of attack, and strike to exposed targets. Restrict your opponent's forward motion by checking his lead knee with your right foot.

As the opponent thrusts down at you, use the bottom of your foot to brush the staff off its intended line of attack.

As you complete the deflecting crescent kick, begin a right strike at the opponent's lead knee. Twist your body sharply into the strike.

As the opponent drops into range, kick him up under his chin with your right foot.

Maintain contact, keeping the opponent checked as you begin to roll up.

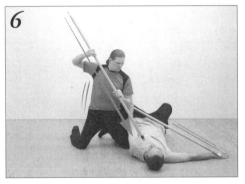

Follow up with a thrust using the heel of the staff.

It is impossible to show every possibility for every situation. Combat is chaotic and many things can happen. Even a small change in timing or position, by either you or your opponent, can make or break a particular technique. Therefore, develop the ability to adapt the concepts introduced here to a variety of situations. To do this successfully you must have a working knowledge of effective strategies and tactics, the wisdom to know how and when to best employ these techniques, and proper training to develop the mental and physical skill sets that will allow you to coordinate your movements into effective combinations of techniques.

These things cannot be explained in detail. From one thing, know ten thousand things. When you attain the Way of strategy, there will not be one thing you cannot see. You must study hard.
—Miyamoto Musashi, *The Book of Five Rings*

Facing Multiple Opponents with the Staff

While fighting a single opponent can be unpredictable, fighting multiple opponents can be downright crazy. Things come at you so fast that there is little time to think, so you will have to rely on superior training and conditioning. Some keys to success are a good understanding of leverage and geometry (see appendix I, "Fighting Physics: The Mechanics of the Staff"), coupled with 360-degree awareness, and knowing how and when to apply a big swing. The staff can buy you a lot of space, but unfortunately you won't always have that luxury. When things get hairy, you will occasionally have to employ close-in levers, pushes, and pokes coupled with good footwork to get yourself out of any tight jams.

A good friend and long-time training partner of mine, Chris Hall (who also happens to be the author of appendix I at the end of this book), wrote to me about a training session he had with some police officer friends of his. In classic form, he had challenged six of them to fight him with a staff. When I read the story, I hoped that someone had recorded a video, but no such luck. But there is still much to be learned from what he wrote back:

No video with the cops, but if I could download what is in my head from that session, you'd laugh. It was classic randori* strategy: flow, line them up to take them down, and don't get caught between them, with ONE exception . . . if you can get them on either side of you, clock them both on the head/follow through on the groin. Occasionally, if that wasn't fast enough and a guy charged in, I'd double punch forward to his chest to check him, then start hitting straight out of basic strikes (1,2,3,4,5,6, etc.) until the next guys entered my defense perimeter. I had them hitting each other with batons a couple of times by breaking to one side after hearing someone rushing up from behind, driving forward into a guy waiting for him to spring back on the attack. Press, press, press, offer a hole/he charges; I duck to the side/he hits partner. One guy tried pepper spray (part of our rules of engagement in that group), and he tagged two other guys when I faded back/staff over head to get behind the two guys and push them by the small of the back into the sprayer. That was a quick 1–2 push to close up the gap in the middle and prevent getting sprayed myself. They were all, except for two of them, level 1–2 fighters, so I spent my time keeping the two experienced guys busy. They both wanted to charge in a little too much, so I used that to my advantage. There was just enough experience in most of them to make them too regimented and predictable. It sounds like a lot of opponents, but in actual, humbling reality this was a two-on-one fight with a lot of useful clutter, and that's all.

*Randori refers to a form of practice in which a designated *aikidoka* (practitioner of aikido) defends against multiple attackers in quick succession without knowing how they will attack or in what order.

I found Chris's account to be typical of my experiences fighting multiple opponents with the staff. This all sounds like a lot to contend with at once, and it is, but with practice you can learn how to manage the chaos.

You can't afford to freeze up when facing off against an angry gang of would-be assailants. The problem is that, if you start with a 50/50 chance of winning against any given opponent, the odds start going down dramatically as additional attackers are added to the scenario. Smart attackers will attempt to surround you in order to attack you from your blind side, minimizing your ability to defend yourself. Therefore, it is important that you keep all of your opponents within your field of vision at all times, or as much as possible. You will want to get out of the "kill zone" they have created as quickly as possible. There are some simple footwork patterns that can help you accomplish these two important objectives.

Let's start with two opponents. Two experienced attackers will usually attempt to get on either side of you, forming a line with you in the middle. You, however, want to be on the end of the line, so that you see them both, can use one opponent to block the approach of the other, and can contend with your opponents one at a time. This strategy is called, "stacking the opponents." You will need to be skilled at smoothly escaping to either side.

Begin from a standard middle grip, allowing you to use both ends of your weapon. Opponent 1, on your left, already sees your body and head as a big open target due to the low position of the heel of your staff on the left side, while the opponent on your right should have a more defensive attitude since he is facing the tip of your staff. Therefore, opponent 1 should be the easier of the two to draw in. Step back and slightly to your left (arrow), off the line of attack, as you lower your guard to draw the left attacker in, while simultaneously increasing the gap between you and the opponent on your right. Evade and parry the incoming strike as you drop your lead foot back and to the left again, moving to the opponent's deadside (in fighting stance, with your right foot back, your deadside is your left side). Continue circling around (arrow) to place opponent 1 between you and opponent 2, all the while being careful never to turn your back to either opponent. Opponent 1 has now become the blocker, preventing opponent 2 from being able to attack you directly.

Begin from a standard middle grip.

Step back off the line of attack.

Evade.

Parry the incoming strike as you drop your lead foot back.

Continue circling to place opponent 1 between you and opponent 2.

Opponent 1 becomes the blocker, preventing opponent 2 from attacking you directly.

This type of situation is constantly changing, and if you do manage to stack your opponents, it is not likely to last very long. Therefore, don't waste the short window of opportunity that you have created. Choose whether to attack or flee (or perhaps attack and *then run* away) quickly, before your opponents can recuperate and reorganize for another attack.

When confronted with three opponents, the concepts are the same. Three attackers will attempt to form a triangle, with you in the middle. Again, you obviously do not want to remain in the center of the kill zone any longer than necessary. Your first priority should be to turn to face one opponent, preferably the one you believe poses the biggest threat to you. This puts the weaker opponents on your flanks and your back to an open side of the triangle. Your next task is to step backward in order to maneuver onto that open side. This will still leave you between two opponents, but two is better than three, and with luck you will find yourself between the two weaker opponents.

We just learned how to escape from the middle of two opponents and attempt to stack them. From one side of the triangle, retreat off the line of attack and see which opponent is more aggressive and follows first. Do not be caught by surprise when the attack comes; it will be fast and hard. Parry the strike as you continue maneuvering out of their circle. Step back a fourth time to put yourself in a strong position facing all of your opponents. If possible, you should take this brief opportunity to quickly flee the scene.

Face the opponent you believe poses the biggest threat to you.

Step backward into an open side of the triangle.

Retreat off the line of attack.

Parry the strike as you continue maneuvering out of the circle.

Flee if possible.

Engaging four or more opponents is, of course, much more challenging, but the strategies and tactics stay pretty much the same as when you engage three. Stay calm and use your brain. The outcome of the situation is totally dependent upon the strategies and tactics you choose to employ.

Another useful technique when dealing with multiple opponents is to swing your staff in full circles at different levels, holding it with one or both hands. This technique can create space for you by causing a group of attackers to spread out, allowing you to deal with them individually rather than as a pack. It is also a useful technique to drive a single opponent back in order to create an opening to escape. Applying the principle of continuation of attack (see level 6), beat or parry the opponent's weapon on the first swing as you close the range, only to circle around to strike again from the same side. As you do this, keep your eyes on the other attackers by turning your body slightly and not looking directly at the opponent you are attacking. Instead, use your peripheral vision to keep track of all your attackers. As the opponent backs up to avoid your attacks, he allows you to advance, momentarily opening the gap between you and the remaining opponents. The big swings also prevent the other attackers from closing on you while you are dealing with the opponent at hand. Ultimately, the resultant change in position should open a hole big enough for you to escape through.

If your attack on your first opponent does not force him to retreat, you will have to quickly switch directions to address the remaining opponent(s) before returning to finish your first opponent. In this way, you should be able to keep the attackers at bay with unpredictable footwork and targeting until you are able to escape from the kill zone.

Jamming: Another strategy is to draw the opponents into attacking by adopting a "come and get me" attitude. Of course, this is just a ruse; you do not actually want them to come get you, so don't get too comfortable.

As soon as one opponent thinks he sees an opening, or gets impatient or overconfident, he will try to close the gap to attack you. As soon as he is committed to his forward movement, you should advance, using sen no sen timing (see "Understanding Timing" in level 6), reclaiming the initiative from the opponent by closing the range faster than expected with an incoming attack of your own.

Stun him with a quick heel strike.

Keep the other opponent in sight as you complete your attack.

Use the heel of your staff to maintain control as you turn to face the remaining opponent.

Quickly take advantage of the opportunity you have created to move to safety.

Multiple-opponent situations are very stressful. Stay calm and keep your head about you; it is your most important tool for survival. Remember the basic strategies of facing the strongest opponent, maneuvering between the weaker two, and stacking them. If you still find yourself unable to maneuver out of the kill zone, you might have to break out of it forcefully. This can be done using a strong, offensive blitz attack, in particular the flèche (see level 6), since it allows you to stun one opponent so you can safely move past him and escape before the others can regroup for another assault.

Flèche Escape: You find yourself surrounded by three opponents with no obvious avenue of escape.

Use a flèche to disable one opponent as you escape. Attack the opponent to your front by feinting a right horizontal strike to draw the opponent into defending his left side.

Flow through with a long but quick step forward into a left heel strike to the right side of the opponent's head.

Your rear foot immediately follows through, stepping behind to move you through the gap, while simultaneously turning you clockwise to face the remaining opponents.

Step your lead foot back to control and maintain the distance between you and the still-active, now-advancing attackers. Note how the neutralized opponent acts as an obstacle impeding their approach. By circling to the left, the defender can keep the injured attacker between him and at least one of the remaining attackers, thereby increasing his odds of surviving the confrontation.

Multiple-opponent fighting may seem excessive or unnecessary training at first; however, let us keep in mind that in true self-defense scenarios, assailants often work in groups to increase their chances of success. You may be as likely to face a gang of armed thugs as you would a single assailant. Therefore, learning how to survive multiple-opponent scenarios should be compulsory training for advanced staff students. While it might be beneficial to work the basic escaping footwork patterns demonstrated above, beginners and novices should refrain from free fighting against multiple opponents until they are more experienced and better able to handle fighting more than one opponent at a time.

In closing, fighting multiple opponents is probably one of the most challenging aspects of combat. Here are some general guidelines you will want to keep in mind:

1. Don't get surrounded. Stay out of the "kill zone." Don't get cornered.

2. Keep all opponents in your field of view. Keep your eyes to the center and use your peripheral vision. Never turn your back to an opponent or let an opponent get behind you.

3. You must control the distance. Keep the opponents at bay by attacking them strategically just as they attempt to close to attack you.

4. In practice we stay and fight to gain experience, but if this were an actual life-and-death situation, you should make every attempt to *flee*, getting yourself and your loved ones to safety as quickly as possible. In short, *run!* If you do have the opportunity to run and the opponents pursue you, faster ones will quickly take the lead as slower or less-motivated opponents lag behind. As your opponents string themselves out, you may be able to engage and quickly dispatch them one at a time as the opportunities present themselves. Don't look for a "fair fight." You want to use deception to your advantage, such as a surprise attack, an ambush, or use of an improvised weapon like slamming a door on someone or throwing a flowerpot at him. Stay calm, think quickly, be resourceful, and make full use of your environment.

> He that fights and runs away, may turn and fight another day;
> but he that is in battle slain, will never rise to fight again.
> —Tacitus

Unarmed Defense against the Staff

Assuming you can't retreat, you may have to face an armed opponent with nothing but your bare hands. While the odds are that you will be hit at least once, you must take control of the opponent's weapon. This can be achieved through good timing, sure footwork, and a warrior mindset. Since a right-to-left diagonal strike is one of the usual methods of attack, there is a very good chance that you can draw a right high strike by leaving your head exposed (see the Three-Step Rule). You must anticipate and correctly read the opponent's attack, then swiftly and smoothly step into the deceleration zone and make contact with the opponent's weapon using *sen sen no sen* timing (see "Understanding Timing" in level 6). At this point, you can apply a hard or a soft finish. A hard-style finish entails disabling the opponent with strikes, while a soft-style response entails using a turning motion to take control of the opponent's weapon and throw him to the ground. Of course, there are many other ways to take a staff away from someone, so I will also include the "bayonet disarm" and "sacrifice throw" to illustrate some further possibilities.

The Hard-Style Approach: Face your opponent in a left stance, rolling the lead shoulder forward to protect your major vital areas. Drop your hands, giving the illusion of an easy target.

When you sense the time is right, preferably at an instant when the opponent loses focus, suddenly bridge the gap and check the weapon with your lead hand.

Grasp the staff and smother the strike as you deliver a right cross.

Immediately grasp the opponent's staff with your free hand.

Use the staff to pull the opponent into a front kick.

Finish with a downward diagonal strike as you strip the staff from your opponent.

The Soft-Style Approach: Adopt a left lead against your armed attacker. This protects you somewhat from right-side strikes coming in from your left. All of your senses must be on high alert, your body relaxed, but ready to explode forward.

As you sense your opponent preparing to attack (using sen sen no sen timing—see "Understanding Timing" in level 6), step through, closing the gap as you raise your right hand to protect your head and intercept the staff.

Grasp the staff as you complete your step, but do not attempt to stop its movement. Instead, allow it to continue its motion as it falls increasingly under your control. Notice that the back foot is already beginning to drift through.

Step you rear foot behind as you continue to rotate the staff.

Continue executing the technique in a single relaxed, fluid motion as his left arm is lifted with the staff.

Pivot to your left just as your left foot comes to rest, using your body weight to drive the technique.

Continue your body rotation to complete the throw.

Do not give the opponent an opportunity to get back to his feet.

Follow up with a thrust with the heel of your staff.

The Bayonet Disarm: Drop your hands, using the Three-Step Rule to draw a thrust from your opponent.

As he thrusts, deftly evade as you parry the tip of his staff over your right shoulder with your left hand.

Reach forward with your right hand.

Grasp the opponent's staff from underneath.

Step back quickly, pulling the opponent forward off his base.

Twist your hips into a downward strike.

The Sacrifice Throw: Face your opponent in a left stance. This turns the tougher outer edges of your body to the most dangerous threat, the tip of his staff, protecting your vital areas as you hover just out of his effective striking range.

As soon as you sense his attack (sen sen no sen timing; see "Understanding Timing" in level 6), step forward with your left foot, closing the gap faster than your opponent expects, which allows you to jam his attack and get hold of his staff.

Bring your right foot in and past your left foot.

Flow into a motion that feels like you are trying to sit on the opponent's foot.

As you lie back, place your right foot on the opponent's lower abdomen.

Lift him into the air.

Kick the opponent over your head with your right leg.

Continue rolling backward, keeping your grip on the staff in order to maintain your position relative to the opponent.

Finish the roll kneeling over the opponent with the staff raised into position, ready to finish the opponent with a downward thrust.

At this point you may be skeptical, and I don't blame you. Could you really disarm someone armed with a staff who is out to do you harm? If you will indulge me for a moment, I would like to tell you a story that may shed some light on the subject.

In 2008, Dave Dickey, founder of Live Steel Fight Academy, Pottstown, Pennsylvania, decided that rather than hosting their annual tournament in the traditional format, he would try something new. The tournament that year consisted only of challenge matches and, at the end of the day, all the fighters voted on the winners. Awards were given for things like "most courageous challenge," "best fight of the day," "biggest upset," and the coveted title "best overall fighter" (which I took home that day, in addition to a few others).

About two months prior to the event, Live Steel Instructor Joe McLaughlin challenged me to a staff match, as did two of my classmates. Since everyone knew the staff was my weapon, they were probably looking to use me to win "biggest upset" or "most courageous challenge," but I thought quickly and turned things around on them. I told my classmates I would accept their challenges, but only if I could take them both on at the same time, to which they readily agreed. When it came to my teacher, Joe, I told him I would accept his challenge, but under the terms that I would start unarmed and take his staff from him, at which point the match would be stopped, he would be given another staff, and then we would continue. I can still hear his reply: "I'd like to see that."

Now, the only problem was that I had never disarmed anyone with a staff before! But my mouth had just written a big check that my butt was going to have to cash, so I started right away. In addition to being a student at Live Steel, I also run my own martial arts school. I still had several weeks before the tourney, and I wasn't going to waste it. Every chance I had, I was giving one of my students a staff and saying, "Attack me!" They almost always used the habitual method of attack, the number-1 strike. Pretty soon, I had a few

reliable techniques worked out and was growing pretty confident in my skills. I was thinking I might actually pull this off, which should be worth something at the tournament. If not, I'd probably win something like "worst beatdown," if you can call that winning.

One night, I was having my black belts attack me with their staves after class. Dawn White was up next, when her fellow black belt, David Martin, saw what I was doing and suggested to her that she feint the first shot a little low, then strike the exposed upper line. So she came at me, and I immediately recognized her load-up for a right midlevel strike. I moved to enter, and just as I got my hand on the staff, she pulled it back slightly, disengaging my hand and immediately taking the upper line. "THWACK!" She nailed me right above my left eye. She immediately stopped attacking and just looked at me, with a shocked expression on her face.

I thought she was just surprised she hit me. I said, "Attack!" She replied, "You're bleeding." I ignored her and yelled, "ATTACK!" At which point she looked at me and said, "You're bleeding . . . badly." I reached up and touched the side of my face, and it was wet with blood. I looked down, and it was dripping onto the mat. So I relented. Even though my wife is an ER nurse at the local hospital, she refused to stitch me up at home, so I had to stop practice for another long, boring visit to the emergency room (not my first, and surely not my last). After that, I had to wear headgear so I wouldn't risk reopening my eye, which was OK because I would have to wear it the day of the tournament anyway (insurance liability blah, blah, blah), so it was good that I got used to it.

On the day of the tournament, my match with my two classmates came up first. I used good footwork to maintain distance and line them up whenever I could. I felt like I was really controlling the match before it went to the ground. Even then, I didn't do too badly. After two minutes of continuous fighting, the match was called a draw. Not long afterward, a big summer storm blew in, and halfway through the event the power went out. The only illumination came in through the glass storefront, which made judging somewhat difficult, but the fights continued . . . in the dark.

When my match with Joe came up, he had his staff, and I stood before him empty handed. I faced off against him with my back to the light, so he was illuminated, and I was backlit. I stood just out of range on the balls of my feet as the referee snapped, "GO!" The tension in the room was thick, and no one breathed in anticipation of what was to come. Up to that point, I was careful to make sure that no one from Live Steel had seen me do my disarm trick, so Joe would be unprepared. He is an excellent fighter, and I knew this could turn bad very quickly. After reviewing the videotape, I could see that he hesitated for only the briefest of moment, but at the time it seemed to me an eternity. Realizing he wasn't moving yet, I sprang forward, grasped his staff, and everyone in the room heard him utter, "Aw, shit!" just before I spun and threw him to the ground. I had gotten lucky, but I had done it. Train hard and, with good timing (and a little luck), you can do it, too.

Do, or do not. There is no try.
—Yoda

LEVEL 9
The Way of the Spear

Intro to the Spear

At the beginning of this book, I mentioned how, in Asia, the staff is considered by many to be the "king of weapons." I propose to you now that the staff is but the prince . . . the true king is the spear. While the staff can hurt, the spear can *kill*.

A spear is simply a staff equipped with a power multiplier, anything from a pointy end to a sharp blade. The importance of the spear lies in its effectiveness and accessibility. Like the staff, the spear is effective against most other weapons because it offers you a greater reach than your opponent, allowing you to attack without putting yourself in as much danger as with a shorter weapon such as a knife, club, or even a sword. While you can't easily carry a spear around with you (let alone conceal one), you could usually improvise one if you needed to. Take almost any long hardwood stick, break one end so that it is pointy, and you have a spear. Given a few common resources (duct tape, a kitchen knife, a broom handle), you can create a very effective improvised home defense weapon in only a matter of minutes.

For best results, go back and repeat all previous levels of training with the spear. You will see that techniques that were effective with a staff are even more so with a spear. In practice, always use dull practice blades, preferably made of rubber, to avoid accidental injuries. When practicing spear techniques with a partner, it is wise to wear some sort of eye protection (such as safety goggles). The best way to do any kind of contact work is to wear protective helmets and use padded spears with thick thrusting tips, large enough that they can't possibly slip through the visor slots on the helmets. That way you can practice much more realistically, with less caution, while gaining important perspective on what a real spear thrust to the face could do to an opponent. Just be sure you use control and take proper precautions!

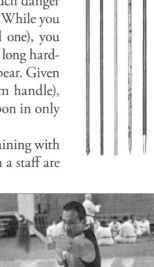

Grandmaster Quynh Ngo of the Cuong Nhu Oriental Martial Arts Association demonstrates a spear thrust.

Basic Spear Fighting Strategy

Fighting with the spear builds on all the other skills you have learned. It is very similar to fighting with the staff in extended grip. The important difference is the addition of a sharp point, and possibly sharp edges as well. Now the weapon is capable not just of inflicting blunt trauma but also of stabbing and cutting.

Basic spear fighting, therefore, is a lot like fencing. A strong strategy can be implemented by fighting from a back stance. Assume a guarded position with your left leg forward and with the tip of your spear pointed at the opponent's chest, anywhere between the navel and the neck. Guard your centerline but don't be static. Move the tip of your spear slowly and irregularly to keep the opponent guessing your next movement. Use footwork to control the distance to ensure your opponent can't close past the tip of your weapon. Keep the opponent just on the right side of your spear. That way, if he does manage to pass the tip, you will still have the shaft of the spear between you to mount a defense. If the opponent passes the tip to the left, you will be vulnerable and exposed to attack.

There are basically two grips with the spear: underhand, with the front hand in the palm-up position, and overhand, with both palms facing down. I find the underhand grip to be better for defensive moves and thrusting, while the overhand grip lends itself more to offensive slashing attacks. For now I will mainly be using the underhand grip, which we are already familiar with through our experience with extended grip staff fighting (see "Advanced Extended Grip" in level 5).

Straight Thrust: From the guard, maintain contact between your weapons to monitor your opponent.

As soon as you detect any movement off the line, thrust forward quickly.

The instant the opponent moves his weapon from his guarding position or otherwise exposes his centerline, you must be ready to thrust forward quickly and decisively, usually accompanied by a shift into forward stance to add reach and power to the attack. As with the staff, thrusts can be made with one hand or two, using either a fixed-hand grip or a slip thrust, depending on the situation. Regardless of the type of thrust, always return to your guarded position immediately after you make your attack.

Of course, you also have all of the techniques from extended-grip staff fighting at your disposal as well, but when sharp points are involved, the ease and effectiveness of the simple straight thrust must be taken into account. Of course, an astute opponent is not just going to let you stab him. You will most likely have to use your fencing skills to create an opening to attack.

Disengage: Your opponent presses against the tip of your spear, attempting to take the centerline.

Disengage, moving your spear in a tight counterclockwise circle and returning to the line on the other side of the opponent's spear tip.

Press his spear slightly to clear a line of attack.

Immediately thrust before the opponent has an opportunity to recover.

Stepping Straight Thrust: Stand seemingly out of range. The opponent, feeling that he is momentarily safe from attack, drops his awareness.

Sensing this, begin stepping forward, being careful to leave the front side of your body as still as possible to avoid telegraphing your attack.

A full step with a single-handed jabbing thrust takes the startled opponent square in the chest.

Training Equipment: The Rings

Here is your opportunity to become the Lord of the Rings (sorry, I just couldn't help myself!). Training rings allow you to develop accurate, penetrating thrusts as well as circular techniques used to manipulate an opponent's weapon. They are useful for training with both staff and spear. The training rings have an additional target, a small wooden disk, suspended in the center.

Training rings can be made from a variety of materials. The ones shown were cut from plywood, then covered in duct tape and hung up with lengths of cord. I used a beat-up old extension cord instead of throwing it away; it is still strong after twenty-plus years and will probably never wear out (in fact, those are the same rings in both pictures). You could also use lengths of old garden hose, duct taped into a circle, to quickly and easily make durable hoops of varying sizes.

Start your practice with the rings stationary. Stand in front of them and thrust your staff or spear through the center without touching the sides. Try to penetrate deeply through the center. Once you can do this well, begin to slowly spin the rings. Your strikes must now be well timed and fast, especially on the withdrawal, to ensure that you do not touch the ring with your weapon. Add footwork to your practice and perhaps even swing the rings as they spin.

You can also practice circles inside the rings, coming close to but not touching the sides. This is good practice for circular techniques such as cutting under an opponent's weapon to take the centerline or for hooking disarms.

Unarmed Defense against a Spear

When facing an opponent with a spear, an unarmed defender will need to get very close in order to attack effectively. Remaining at the spearman's range puts the unarmed defender at a great disadvantage, as the defender can be struck while the spearman remains safely out of range.

The unarmed defender must rely on cunning to lure his attacker into making a mistake. Using the Three-Step Rule, it is possible to draw an attack by standing square to the opponent, leaving your body exposed to a straight thrust. When the thrust comes, the defender must evade the tip of the spear and grasp the shaft to control the weapon. He can then enter to combat the attacker on more even terms.

Defending against the Spear: Stand square to the opponent, giving him a target he cannot resist, but be ready to "open the door" at any instant because when the attack comes, it will come quickly.

As the opponent thrusts at your midsection, shift your weight to your right foot as you pivot your body counterclockwise to get off the opponent's intended line of attack.

As soon as you grasp the weapon, press upward with your right hand and downward with your left, levering the opponent's end of the spear upward slightly.

Twist sharply to your left to bring your opponent to the ground.

If you are the spearman and your weapon is seized, you must know how to free it quickly. As soon as you feel the opponent's hands grasp your spear, thrust the tip forward forcefully, possibly resulting in a stab. Immediately retract the weapon, stepping backward as you do so to get your body weight into the technique.

The Push-Pull Defense: Stab at the open midsection of your opponent.

He sidesteps your thrust and grabs the shaft of your spear.

Quickly pull the spear back toward you, cutting his hands.

Circle Escape: The opponent grasps your spear with only one hand, or you have just managed to partially disarm him.

Take advantage of the fact that you have much greater leverage since you still have both hands on the spear.

Circle the tip clockwise under the opponent's wrist.

Continue the rotation.

Strip his hand from the shaft.

Strike the adversary.

If the first maneuver does not successfully free your weapon, you should take advantage of the fact that the opponent's attention is now likely going to be concentrated on the weapon, and quickly apply a low stamping kick to his knee. This should at least check his forward progress by preventing him from stepping forward. At best, you could hyperextend or break his knee joint, which should encourage him to release the weapon.

You can stomp on the opponent's knee with either leg, from the front or side.

Keep in mind that you should follow up with a slash or stab to quickly incapacitate the opponent. If he gets his hands on your weapon again, you may not be so lucky.

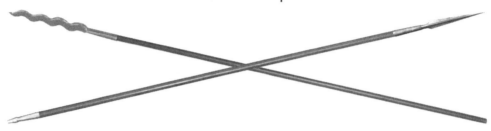

Quality is never an accident, it is always the result of high intention, sincere effort, intelligent direction, and skillful execution; it represents the wise choice of many alternatives.
—Dr. Frank Spear

Throwing the Spear

One important advantage of the spear is that it can serve equally well as a handheld weapon or as a projectile. Of course, as with all strategies, there are some important advantages and disadvantages to throwing your spear.

The advantages include increased range, increased power, and the element of surprise. The hand-thrown spear is silent, has an accurate range of about thirty feet or so, and can be very effective, especially when suddenly and unexpectedly thrown at an opponent from nearly point-blank range. As for power, Lynn C. Thompson, founder of Cold Steel, Inc., and an avid spear hunter, perhaps summed it up best when he wrote, *"Penetration of a hand thrown spear through flesh and bone rivals that produced by a 470 Nitro Elephant Rifle. A good spearman can easily hurl his spear completely through a bull elk, moose, grizzly bear, or even a cape buffalo."*

The obvious disadvantage of throwing your spear is that if you miss and the spear was your only weapon, you had best get running because the opponent is coming after you, and now he has your spear! However, you may choose to throw your spear to create an opening in order to close in on the opponent, quickly rushing in behind it as soon as the spear leaves your hand. Of course, if you have time to prepare, you might be able to fashion several spears, keeping one for defense while throwing the others.

The first step in throwing any spear is to find the balance point on the shaft by resting it horizontally across your open palm. Hold the spear with your thumb facing in the opposite direction from the point. Once you have determined the balance point, grasp the weapon loosely, being careful not to wrap your fingers completely around the shaft. Hold the spear close to your head, keeping it parallel to the ground and using your wrist as a pivot.

Rest the staff horizontally across your open palm to find the balance point.

Hold the spear with your thumb facing in the opposite direction from the point.

Grasp the weapon loosely. Hold it close to your head, keeping it parallel to the ground.

Hold your spear loosely parallel to the ground, by your head, using the grip described above. Point the tip directly at your target as you pull your hand back slightly. Push off your rear leg as you rotate your body into the throw. Extend your arm as far as possible before releasing the spear, at which point only your thumb and index finger will be holding it. Your throwing arm should stay centered on the target, not your own centerline. Therefore, if you are centered on the target and doing a right-handed throw, the weapon will necessarily travel slightly to your left in order to hit the target. You must keep the entire shaft straight and aligned with the target throughout this motion in order to ensure a stable and accurate throw.

Hold your spear loosely parallel to the ground.

Point the tip directly at your target as you pull your hand back slightly.

Keep your throwing arm centered on the target, not your own centerline.

Push off your rear leg as you rotate your body into the throw.

Keep the entire shaft straight and aligned with the target to ensure a stable and accurate throw.

At distances of less than twenty feet you can throw the spear pretty much flat and level into the target, giving the opponent very little time to evade your attack. However, to reach targets at greater distances, you will have to throw your spear slightly upward, which allows it to arc down and into the target, giving the opponent more time to take evasive action.

Practice throwing your spear into a soft target such as a bale of hay. Even then, throwing your good spear will certainly shorten its lifespan. Luckily, you can make an inexpensive yet durable practice thrower from something as simple as a rake handle with a short length of rebar inserted into the tip as a point.

Catching the Spear

This might fall under the heading "unarmed defense against a spear," as you would not be likely to employ this strategy if you already had a spear in your hands, opting instead for the safer motion of parrying the opponent's throw. I could imagine a scenario, however, where you might be unarmed or have a shorter, inferior weapon, with the opponent attempting to engage you, but you keep evading and staying out of range. The frustrated opponent throws his weapon at you, at which point you unexpectedly catch the spear and turn the tables on your startled opponent.

While this seems far-fetched at first, with some practice it is quite possible. Like new feats of athletics, some things seem impossible until one person does it, and soon it seems that many others can accomplish the same feat. Part of the trick is the realization that such a technique *can* be done.

Through learning how to throw the spear, you will also learn to expect it and see the signs should the strategy be used against you. If you do successfully see the telegraphing movements that lead into a throw, you may be able to counter by catching the spear. First, follow the Three-Step Rule by giving your opponent a target he cannot resist, standing square but well out of reach. As the opponent throws, wait until he is committed to the attack. Once the weapon leaves his hand he has reached the point in his throw where he can no longer change the trajectory of his attack, and you may start your movement.

Stay calm and keep your eyes on the opponent's release and the path of the incoming weapon. As the spear leaves his hand, "open the door" by swinging one foot back into line with your lead foot, turning your body back and off the line of attack as you quickly calculate the trajectory of the incoming weapon. With practice and good timing you can grab the shaft as the weapon goes by. With a quick twirl to redirect and bring the momentum of the weapon under control, you can quickly spin the spear into position to guard, attack, or throw it back.

Stand square but well out of reach.

Grab the shaft of the spear as the weapon goes by.

Swing one foot back, turning your body off the line of attack.

Twirl the spear to redirect it and bring the momentum of the weapon under control.

Guard, attack, or throw the spear back.

Through learning how to throw the spear, you will also learn to expect it and see the signs should the strategy be used against you. If you do successfully see the telegraphing movements that lead into a throw, you may be able to counter by catching the spear.

This entire process can be best summed up in the classic samurai maxim:

To know and to act are one and the same.

Tub Tilting

(Author's re-creation)

Ready for a new activity to spice up your staff and spear training? While serious practice is essential to success, so is adding an element of fun. Here is an oldie but goodie from *How to Do Things,* a compendium of practical crafts and fun games published for boys and girls by *The Farm Journal* in 1919.

Secure two barrels, about flour-barrel size, and two poles. Each pole should be from eight to ten feet long, of the lightest possible wood, with a big soft pad on the end. These are spears for attacking. The barrels are set level, exactly at poles' length apart, center to center. Each contestant takes his place on a barrel, and he must try to put the other fellow off. The umpire stands alongside, near the middle. For safety's sake it is a good idea to have someone stand behind each player to act as a catcher in case of accident.

It is counted a foul to push the other player below the knees, to use the spear as a club, to push the barrel, or to take hold of your opponent's spear with your hand. A foul gives the round to the other boy. A round is up when one boy goes off his barrel.

If one drops his spear and can recover it without getting or falling off, it is all right.

A battle usually lasts for about seven or eight rounds. The best players gain their points by wriggling their bodies and keeping in continual motion.

There is a lot of fun and excitement in keeping your balance.

Safe "boffer spears" (a boffer is a padded weapon) should have light shafts and nice thick striking tips made up of several disks of dense foam glued one on top of the other and covered with smooth tape.

The good old game of "tub tilting" holds a lot of potential for helping you in your current training. Start by replacing those long poles with padded staffs or spears with sufficiently padded striking tips. Instead of big barrels you could use tree stumps, logs planted in the ground, or upside-down five-gallon buckets. Be creative!

I like to practice on "gongfu stumps." Sometimes we move and use all the stumps, while other times players have to stand on just one. Sometimes we can only thrust, while at other times anything goes. Just agree on the rules beforehand to avoid any unnecessary misunderstandings!

We also fight on a raised balance beam, really just a long board nailed across two stumps, that we call the "fighting board." Both training tools will improve your balance and enhance your development of strategy and tactics. Whatever equipment you choose to use, be smart and keep the safety of all participants foremost in your mind.

Each game has its own particular rules, which can always be changed as need, opportunity, or whim arises. The point is to become more versatile with your weapon, more knowledgeable of strategy, more flexible in your training, and, above all, to have *fun!*

A board nailed across some stumps can add a challenging aspect to your staff fighting.

Appendix I

Fighting Physics: The Mechanics of the Staff

by Chris Hall

Physics is one broad brushstroke of a topic! If we got technical, we could talk about how the atoms of the staff and the arrangement of the wood fibers along its length give the staff its unique characteristics, capabilities, and combat effectiveness. A stack of firewood set aside for a winter evening's discussion, even a discussion touching only the basics, would be long gone before we scratched the surface.

To pare down this section into something more manageable (and practical), let's focus on mechanics. Mechanics is a branch of physics that deals with motion, and all the larger facets of staff fighting are rooted in motion: striking, blocking/parrying, and levering. Even the footwork in staff fighting involves setting up ideal pathways for the transmission of force and leverage through these motions.

In the next few pages, we will unpack the mechanics behind striking, blocking/parrying, and levering, while providing some diagrams and experiments to incorporate the basics into your intuitive practice and muscle memory.

The bottom line is that a proper understanding of mechanics will help you gain a properly informed *feel* for the staff. If you use the technical explanations to gain understanding, then use your understanding to guide practice, then practice diligently and ceaselessly to cultivate intuition, you will develop the ability to respond wisely—not simply react quickly—to the inevitable surprises in staff fighting.

The Big Three

If you want to get to the bottom line of striking and blocking right away, then there are three complementary concepts you should know:

1. Newton's Second Law of Motion, or $F = ma$

2. Momentum and impulse, or $Ft = \Delta mv$

3. Kinetic Energy, or $KE = 1/2mv^2$, and Work, or $W = Fd$

Newton's Second Law of Motion states the relationship between force (F), mass (m), and acceleration (a). Newton said that force equals mass times acceleration ($F = ma$), and you could interpret that two ways since you can read the equation from right to left or from left to right: when you receive a force, you are receiving a mass that has been accelerated toward you, and when you want to accelerate something, you will need to generate force to set its mass in motion.

Now, if force can accelerate mass, we have to wonder whether time has an effect. Think about pushing a car with a bad starter: you lean into the back bumper of that old Chevette while your friend steers, and it starts to roll. The longer you lean into it, assuming you're still on a flat surface, the faster it rolls. Accelerating mass to a certain velocity, or speed in a particular direction, involves applying force to it for a certain length of time. At a given moment, we could measure how fast and in what direction the ol' beast is rolling, and that would give us its velocity.

A second equation, $Ft = \Delta mv$, expresses the relationship between force and time, on the one hand, and mass and velocity on the other. Ft is force times time and that Δ (Greek delta) means "change," so the longer you apply force (Ft), the greater the change will be in the velocity of a mass. Football linemen are taught to drive through their opponents in order to keep them moving back, back, back. To train for this, they don't hit the sled in practice and then stop pushing. Rather, they use a constant force over a longer period of time to move their opponents back at a faster and faster rate.

Finally, it's also important to be able to talk about forces in terms of work and energy. Work involves force applied to a resisting object, like your opponent's weapon or body, which does not want to move. The more you move that object, the more work you are doing. In mechanics, we use the word "work" a little differently than in daily conversation: since $W = Fd$, where W is work, F is force, and d is distance, unless you're covering d, you're not really doing any work. I know a lot of desk jockeys who might disagree with this, but physics has its own opinions on the matter.

We all know that to do work, energy is required. We have to eat in order to keep working, and we know that we have to contract muscles in order to move our bodies. In other words, we have stored energy, or potential energy, in our bodies from food and muscular tension. In order to do work on our resisting opponent and his weapon, we have to change that potential energy into kinetic energy, or energy in motion.

At this point, let's dive right into striking, for there is no better way to illustrate the finer points of *KE* than to start swinging.

Striking

On an episode of National Geographic Channel's *Fight Science,* a television show dedicated to applying laboratory techniques to the study of the martial arts, they demonstrated that the staff can strike with an amazing 2,769 pounds of force, more than twice that of a short stick strike. This is because the staff has more mass and, like a bicycle tire, the tip is moving faster than the center of rotation. At three times the length of a traditional eskrima stick, the staff travels a much greater distance to the target in roughly the same amount of time. More mass moving at a greater speed results in more momentum and more impact on the target.

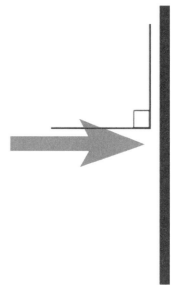

Remember: *Fast and right for striking tight.*

By that, I mean

1. Strike as fast as you can because that maximizes the kinetic energy of your strike,

and

2. Strike at a *right angle* to your target surface in order to maximize energy transfer.

Kinetic Energy

Think about a compressed spring. That is an image of stored energy, waiting to be released. Stored energy is called **potential energy**, and you have it in your muscles, through the miracles of chemistry and biology, and as the calories in food. When you "burn" those chemicals, you release their stored energy as **kinetic energy**, or energy in motion.

You can maximize the kinetic energy transfer into an object or opponent, the power of your strike, by maximizing mass in motion and velocity.

Mass is more than weight. It is the actual amount of matter in an object. To visualize, consider a pebble and a small boulder. Assuming they're made out of the same type of rock, the boulder will have more mass than the pebble: it simply has more rock in it.

Which would you rather have fall on your foot? If you answered "the boulder," then I suggest you put this book down, perform the experiment, and get back to me about the results. If you said "the pebble," then you have an intuitive understanding that the resulting pain of impact will be less with the less-massive object.

With mass in mind now, let's consider the way a physicist actually *calculates* kinetic energy, because the mathematics will illustrate an important point about the relationship between mass and velocity. We just said that mass in motion is important, but $KE = 1/2mv^2$.

This means that *kinetic energy equals one half of the mass times the velocity,* or how fast an object is going in a particular direction, *squared*. Not just "increased" or even doubled, but squared.

Consider that pebble and boulder problem again. If I asked you again which you wanted to fall on your foot, but I said that for this trial you would drop the boulder from knee height onto your foot, but that you would fire the pebble out of a pistol at your foot, giving it a lot more velocity than the trial before, then I wouldn't fault you for choosing the more massive of the two.

In summary, striking as fast as you can with precision, with as much mass in motion as you can muster, will give you the hardest hit.

Dynamics

It is worth noting that striking isn't always about generating the hardest hit. Consider the techniques in this book. Sometimes you simply want to tap a target in order to draw the opponent's mind to that point. Sometimes you want to come in fast . . . and then switch direction for the real strike that you just feinted for.

A good musician will tell you that **dynamics** are vitally important to performance. It's not always about playing the notes loud or soft, it's about mixing those two up in such a way that you lead the listener into the song through the spectrum of loud and soft that you play as you go. So, too, with striking. Learn to control the dynamics of your strikes to lead the opponent exactly where you want her to go.

Angle of Impact

Remember: *right makes might.*

We've all been in snowball fights, so I'll use one to illustrate this maxim. Remember the times that you've been hit in the face with a snowball? Which hurts more, the glancing blow that grazed your cheek, only to rile you up that much more, or the one that caught you square between the eyes and dropped you on the spot?

Consider car collisions. Which does more damage to the occupants, the sideswipe or the head-on?

When you want to impart the most kinetic energy to a target, you have to impact that target at a right angle. Anything else and the energy will be dissipated in directions other than one you want.

Come to the lab: hang a heavy bag and run the following experiment to see just how much energy can be lost as the striking angle moves further and further from 90 degrees. First, strike at 90 degrees and listen to the sound of the impact. Note the movement of the bag and the lack of slide or play between the staff and the bag surface. Next, mirroring the velocity of the first strike, strike the bag again at about a 60-degree angle. Up or down, it doesn't matter. Note the decreased movement of the bag: less energy was transferred into the bag from your strike. Note, too, the way the staff slides against the bag surface, dissipating the energy of your strike in a harmless, sideways motion. Try this again at 45 degrees to the bag surface, then again at 30 degrees or less. If you keep the velocity and body mechanics of your strike the same, except for the angle, you will notice the diminishing return of energy transfer.

Notice, too, that you will tend to compensate reflexively. You will find yourself dropping your body weight into the strike if you're striking down, just to retain the power. You may notice an uppercut structure starting to take over as you strike up, a reflex to keep your hips in the power arc. This is natural and good: it shows that you have the instinct to compensate for a less-than-desirable angle by maximizing other elements of the kinetic transfer. What is best to cultivate, however, is the deep awareness of the right angle in striking: it optimizes all the elements of the hit.

For the staff, right makes might.

Striking Surface: Smaller Is Better

When striking, it is also important to consider the size and shape of the striking surface.

Force applied to an area will be dispersed across the *entire* area. If you strike with a similar force, the strike that spreads that force across a larger area will be dissipated, and will not cause as much localized damage as a strike that concentrates force in a small area.

Consider splitting a piece of wood. Which part of the axe would you use first, the hammer-like backside or the blade? One of the simplest machines in the world, the wedge, is the reason that you're going to default to the sharpened blade: assuming a similar amount of force applied, a wedge-shaped edge will part the material you're cutting into more efficiently because it concentrates force along a small area, the width of the blade edge itself, while the back of the axe head dissipates your force over a much wider area.

Staves come in many configurations. Tapered and toothpick staves can improve speed due to decreased mass. Non-tapered staves can provide better strength and durability when blocking. However, octagonal or faceted staves can provide piercing strikes due to their edges, which concentrate and amplify your force.

In fact, concentration of force is the key to destructive power in your strikes. To illustrate this, let's look at three different hypothetical strikes, each delivered with the same force and body mechanics. The only difference will be the striking surface. First, strike a target with the last six inches of your staff. Assuming you are using a staff that is 1 inch wide, the result is a striking surface that is roughly 6 inches square ($6 \times 1 = 6$). For the sake of easy computation, let us say you struck with 60 pounds of pressure. Divide that 60 pounds by the 6 square inches: you are hitting with ($60 \div 6 = 10$), and you will find that you have stuck with only 10 pounds of pressure per square inch (PSI). That's not very destructive.

Strike again, only now reduce your impact zone to the top three inches of the staff. Divide the same 60 pounds by 3 square inches and you are now hitting with 20 pounds of pressure per square inch ($60 \div 3 = 20$), doubling the power of your strike. We're getting better.

Strike a third time, but this time hit with only the tip of the staff, let's say one square inch. The math is easy ($60 \div 1 = 60$): you are now striking with *60* pounds of force per square inch. That's *six times* harder than your original strike, and all you've done is minimize the surface area you are striking with. Maximum results with minimal effort!

Blocking and Parrying

The difference between blocking and parrying is equivalent to the difference between stopping and sliding. **Blocking implies that you bring the opponent's weapon to a standstill, while parrying means that you shift the course of your opponent's weapon while it remains in motion.**

Some of you may have flashed back to high school physics just now because of that deliberate, if partial, quote from famous physicist, mathematician, professor, and let's not forget, alchemist, Sir Isaac Newton. In the first of his three laws of motion, the **Law of Inertia,** Newton states that an object at rest will remain at rest, and an object in motion will remain in motion at a constant velocity unless acted upon by an unbalanced force. That law tells us a lot about effective blocking and parrying: you need to either bring an opponent's weapon to rest or place enough force on it to make it shift course from its intended target.

An important concept to recall here is **momentum,** which is the product of the mass of an object (m, for mass) and how fast it is going in a particular direction (v, for velocity).

Momentum = mv

We know about momentum almost instinctively. No one wants to get hit by a car. Why not? Because a moment's thought will bring to mind some time in our lives when we have been struck by objects that are both larger and faster moving than ourselves at the time. A large dog when we were kids, a large friend when we were in high school, or later in life, a large, hyperactive first grader not watching where he is going. It doesn't take long to run the thought experiment required to see that being struck by even a slow-moving car would be unpleasant.

To bring that thought to bear on blocking, in order to stop an object, all you need to do is match its momentum. Sounds easy! And it is in most circumstances, but the mechanics of doing so quickly and efficiently are pretty precise: you either have to meet that incoming force head on with a perfectly matched equal and opposite force, *or* you have to become a kinetic energy absorber that brings the opponent's weapon to a standstill by sapping it of its momentum. In other words, *you need to become an immovable object or a wet towel.*

The Wall

Let's be real. When you're in a fight and the adrenalin is flowing, you will not have time (or available neurons or fine motor control) to block by setting your angles so precisely that you meet and match your opponent's repeated, nontelegraphed strikes. You will have time to get your staff in position to receive a strike and then play off of the results. **As such, it's good to think of blocking as simply putting a wall between you and an opponent.** A wall that will not move and that will not buckle when struck.

The characteristics that make a wall immovable are a firm foundation, a lot of mass, and a cohesive structure. Your staff has cohesion in spades: most wood fibers are very cohesive. So to maximize the first two characteristics, *you will need to set your body structure so that anything that strikes your staff will transfer momentum to your entire well-rooted, and thus hard-to-move, mass.*

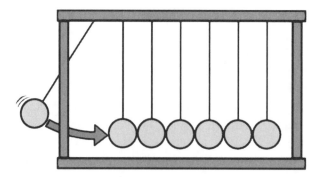

Forces being transferred to you will ultimately find a stopping point in the earth via the bottoms of your feet. Think about the famous desktop toy Newton's Cradle. When you release the ball at one end, only the ball at the far end flies away; the rest of the balls in the line remain at rest. If you imagine your opponent's strike as the starter ball, you can think of your foot/earth connection as the end ball. The difference for the staff fighter is that our mass presses against the earth, and the earth is an object that will tend to remain (relative to us) *very much* at rest no matter how much human force gets transferred to it.

To be an effective wall, you will also need to use your mass as a momentum absorber and your skeleton as a framework for force transmission. To illustrate what I mean, you may notice that in basic block 5, the staff is being supported by your two arms working together and thus dividing the force of the impact evenly between them, rooting it through your spine and the stationary mass of your torso, then down through your legs and into the earth. In block 6, however, your arms continue to work together to divide the force, and your body weight provides the momentum drop necessary to stop the opponent's weapon cold. An upward strike cannot impart enough force to your body to overcome its inertia, and so you stay put.

It is important to note that your arms have to be straightened but not locked to perform these blocks: your muscles take *some* of the force out of the opponent's strike by absorbing it elastically, stretching and returning to shape, and thus robbing energy from the strike.

To practice the skills of rooting and proper body structure, head back to the heavy bag. Press on the bag with your staff at different angles while holding the staff in middle grip, then again while holding it in extended grip. See if you can feel the pressing at the bottom of your feet that matches your pressure on the bag. If you can feel the connection between the two, you can be assured you are rooted properly to receive a force equivalent to what the bag is exerting upon you. Karateka know this sensation from the makiwara: projecting into and through the target is only possible while the feet are rooted to the ground.

To practice good body structure to receive a strike, set the bag in motion, then stop it as it swings back to you. Take video of yourself doing this if you can. You can both hear and feel if your structure is good: the satisfying thud of a now-motionless bag; the minimal amount of movement in your body as you receive its momentum and stop it cold. Watching the video will give you some good feedback about how well you did. Be sure to watch your feet: if they slide, you're leaking force in your counter.

The Wet Blanket (and Subsequent Counterattack)

The other way to stop a strike is to be a wet blanket, sapping the strike of momentum by bleeding it out over a few moments of continued movement. The way to accomplish this is to give a little as the strike comes in. Don't lose your structure, just let it expend some momentum moving your weight for a brief moment . . . into a position of coiled readiness. Then counterattack. Remember: your opponent knows that a stopped staff is no longer pressing the attack, and he will likely shift to a new line of attack immediately.

Pulsing back after a block can be a useful technique. Use that same structure that just received momentum to impart some back. Your muscles are coiled from giving a little, so let them pop back to normal, borrowing the energy of the opponent's strike to energize your own. If your opponent's structure is poor because he has overextended himself in the strike or has lost his footing, you have a good chance of keeping him from regaining his base if you pulse back while he is overextended, limiting his ability to both attack and defend. That's your opportunity to counter.

Parrying

Unlike blocking, you're not trying to stop your opponent's weapon outright when you parry. Rather, you're letting it continue moving after shifting its course away from you. Parrying can often be used to change range or angle to your advantage since it takes a moment for your opponent to change the momentum of his weapon to match the new situation (remember: as Newton explained, that weapon wants to keep going in its original trajectory at its original velocity).

To parry, you need structure, but not the rootedness demanded by outright blocking. Since you're not stopping the momentum coming in but simply redirecting it, you can parry by providing enough structure that the opponent's weapon changes course. Side-stepping a basic strike 5, letting your opponent's staff slide down yours and away from your centerline, is a great example of structure without unnecessary rootedness: you could perform this parry flat-footed or while charging in to close range.

To practice parrying with the heavy bag, set the bag in motion by pushing it with your staff, then parry it as it swings back to you. You will notice that footwork is vital to success.

Levers

Besides striking and blocking, your staff makes an excellent lever. Leverage can be used to uproot opponents or to maximize your force when you want to push something (or someone) over with your staff.

In order to understand levers, you have to know which parts of the lever are moving and which are stationary. Think of a seesaw, which is a form of lever called a first-class lever. There is a stationary pivot at the center called the **fulcrum.** The fulcrum does not move. If it did, you can imagine how the seesaw would lose its fun factor, not to mention its insurance coverage.

The seesaw works best when the two kids at either end are of the same weight, since that means they can both easily propel one another up and counterbalance each other on the way down. In technical terms that we will revisit later, the weight to be moved (the kid on the ground waiting to go up) is the load, and the force put into moving her (the kid waiting in the air for gravity to take over) is called the effort. If the weights are equal, the load and the effort required to make the seesaw go are also equal, and everyone has an easy time of it.

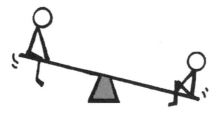

Now, if an NFL lineman decides to take a turn on one end while keeping the same kid on the other, then you will see a fine experiment in unequal forces. The earth's downward pull on the lineman on one side of the lever becomes a large upward push for the kid, who is now enrolled in flight school. Similarly, if the lineman somehow starts in the down position, the effort required to lift him will be more than the earth's pull on the girl now left hanging helplessly in the air.

First-class or seesaw-type levers seldom appear in staff fighting, but they illustrate the mechanics behind some that do. Fulcrums, loads, and efforts describe the mechanics in two other kinds of levers that appear often in staff techniques, especially in uproots and pushes. Technically, they are known as second-class and third-class levers, respectively, but maybe they'll be remembered more easily if we call them the uprooting lever and the pushing lever.

Uprooting Lever (Second-Class Lever)

The uprooting lever can be seen in a well-known garden implement, the wheelbarrow. The fulcrum on a wheelbarrow is the front axle. Even though the wheel rotates, the axle of that wheel remains a fixed bar, with no change in height relative to the ground as you roll along. The contents in the barrow represent the load, and your pulling up on the two handles represents the effort. The fact that the load is between the effort and the fulcrum makes it easier to lift: you're not lifting that weight straight up, but rather in a shorter arc than the one your hands travel through. Shorter distance for the load to travel = less work for the lifter. You can pack a lot of weight in a wheelbarrow and move it with a lot less effort than if you stuck with a lift-and-carry method.

The same mechanics show up in an uproot. When you shoot the tip of your staff between your opponent's legs to plant it on the ground behind him, your staff tip becomes a fulcrum. Your opponent is now the load, and you provide the effort to lift him. With a push up on your end, you can transfer the force of your lift up and through your opponent's pelvis, lifting him just like a load of compost.

Note that when you perform an uproot, some of the force will be transferred *up* while some force will be transferred *forward* through your opponent. This has to do with the fact that the fulcrum is set so far below the opponent's center of mass that as you push the staff toward a vertical position, his mass will tend to slide down the shaft of the staff as well as be driven up. This means that you need to maximize the upward force quickly! Give your opponent a quick uproot to break his base, then follow through immediately.

To gain a deeper understanding of the best placement for an uprooting lever, head back to the heavy bag. Place a staff tip about six inches behind the bag as it hangs. That's your fulcrum. Next, line the rest of your staff up with the middle of the bag's underside. Now test the effort needed to lift the hanging bag up, and note the amount of forward projection you experience. Reset the fulcrum so that it is now a foot behind the bag and try again. Then again at 1.5 feet, 2 feet, and so on, until you get to a point where levering would be impractical because you are bending over so much to do it. Under which conditions did you get the best vertical lift? Forward push? And under which conditions would you say an uprooting lever would work best for a particular size of opponent?

Try this same experiment with a partner. Note: wear a cup for this one! The line that must be considered is called the "balance line" that runs perpendicular to a line running between your opponent's heels.

Place the staff tip six inches behind your cooperative opponent and uproot him. Try again at 1 foot behind him, then 1.5 feet, then 2 feet, and so on until you are bending over too far to make this a practical technique. Discuss the results. Let him try this on you. Any differences noted? If you are of very different heights, you should notice one right away. If you are of different builds, with different centers of mass and different skeletal structures, you may notice others. Try this drill with as many willing partners as you can find so that you will instinctively know the best depth and setup for any opponent.

Pushing Lever (Third-Class Lever)

An example of a third-class lever is one side of a pair of tweezers. In this case, the fulcrum is at one end of the lever, the load is at the opposite end, and the force is applied somewhere along the length of the lever.

Notice how this differs from the second-class lever illustrated by the wheelbarrow. The position of the force and load are reversed, and so it becomes easier to exert a larger force at the load end, with a smaller movement or force at a point along the length of the lever. That force multiplication is what makes the third-class lever the best choice when pushing an opponent into a position of advantage.

In some cases, like when you notice a tripping hazard that your opponent doesn't see, one you want him to fall over, you might not want to hit hard and fast, but rather push him toward the hazard. The feel of this contact isn't "pop" as much as "puuuuuush," with a longer period of contact and, therefore, force transmission. The feel is less like a tackle and more like a lineman's drive into an opponent.

A physicist will tell you that changing an opponent's momentum involves imparting the greatest possible force for the longest possible time. Remember $Ft = \Delta mv$ from the beginning of this appendix? This is why even small objects dropped from tall buildings can become deadly missiles: the tug of gravity never relents for all those seconds of free fall, which means that the object continues to accelerate until only air resistance is slowing it down. Given a longer distance and no air resistance, you could achieve mind-bending velocities, like the 50–60 miles *per second* comets often reach as they fall all the way from the edges of our solar system to the sun.

In staff fighting we don't have gravity working with us like that, but we do have leverage. **The fulcrum for a pushing lever is *you*. You have to be rooted to the ground, and you have to have structure behind your push.** Connect the staff to your pelvis to link it with your center of mass, making your push that much harder to resist. Trying to push with your arms alone results in a collapsed structure and less force transmitted, neither of which sets you up for success.

It is important to note that the effort in the pushing lever comes from your body pivoting through and from your moving forward, *not* from your hands. Your hands are simply transmitters for the rest of your body's rotational energy. As you turn, your lead hand sets the height at which the effort will be transmitted to the load, your opponent. If you want to push him from a high point, your lead hand will be up, but if you want to push him from the midsection, it will be lower. Either way, the bend of the front arm should not exceed 120 degrees, for the same reason that a boxer's hook shouldn't: angled any further, the arm will lose power transmission from the hips. Don't reach for a push; it ruins your structure. Instead, buy ground with some quick footwork.

One more consideration: **Don't push *to*, push *through*.** One important piece of advice for *tameshiwari*, or breaking of objects with the bare hands in karate, is to aim *behind* the objects you want to break. If you aim to your point of contact alone, you will not transmit enough force through the objects to break them. Aiming behind those objects primes the mind and the body to project force through to that point, setting up the structure it takes to be successful. In staff fighting, this translates to stepping into the push a bit, projecting your mass forward and into your opponent through the far end of your staff. If you can project in at the same time that your opponent is falling back or caving in structurally, then you've got him. Interrupt his space with your mass and he can't occupy it again.

To get a feel for this, revisit the heavy bag. Stand in front of, but slightly to the right side of, the bag in an extended basic strike-5 position. Your right hand should be on the bag side of your body. Set the left-hand end of your staff in your center of mass just above the left crest of your pelvis. Let your right hand travel forward of your pelvis about six inches until the right tip of your staff contacts the bag. Don't hit, just contact; remember, we're aiming for push mechanics. Notice that this angle, with the staff slightly farther ahead of your body on the right, will give you a better push in a moment.

With your left foot slightly forward, start to pivot your body, driving your body weight into the bag. If your structure is solid, you will notice that the bag is relatively easy to push. If not, adjust your hand position and posture until it feels easy. The feel you're aiming for is that your body rotation can displace the bag without effort. Once you have it in this position, switch to the other side of the bag and try again. Try at other angles too, keeping in mind the advantageous anatomy of an opponent; for example, a push up through the kidneys toward the tip of the sternum successfully uproots and moves an opponent into a wall.

The Kinetic Chain

In ancient China, there was a sage named Ssu Ma. He was renowned both for his book learning and for his wisdom, and his students were treated daily to lectures and talks on subject upon subject. While his students were young, they found him remarkably easy to follow, and they marveled at his ability to impart to them the deepest nuances and subtleties of disciplines. One day a student spoke up and asked, "Master, how is it that you know so much?"

Ssu Ma answered, "My student, where you see all the disciplines as so many separate studies, I link all upon a single thread."

One of the dangers of reading about the mechanics of the staff is that, as you train, you may lose the whole in the sum of the parts. While it is good to break down strikes, blocks, and parries into their constituent levers, rooting structures, and physical elements, it is vitally important to understand that these elements are working, always and forever, in concert. No one element will hold sway, but all elements are important in creating a fully functional *kinetic chain:* a series of maximized kinetic energy outputs linked together and focused on a single, small-area point of contact.

If the elements of staff mechanics are algebra, born of logic and simple equations, then the *totality* of staff mechanics is calculus; measuring the whole of any technique requires a summation of its elements. Thus the concept of the kinetic chain: all the elements along the full curve of the strike, block, or parry must be maximized in a coordinated manner in order to achieve the greatest kinetic output.

Consider the mechanics of a basic number-1 strike alone. As you begin the strike, the fulcrum of the staff is at the midpoint of the weapon, but as the swing advances, the fulcrum slides somewhat toward the rear hand as the arms extend. The body drops and the muscles of the left leg coil with potential energy for the next strike. The left arm provides a physical support at a certain point in the arc as the staff comes to rest against the triceps, and yet this contact should not be hard enough to rob the staff of momentum. In reality, the power arc of even the most basic strike is a stew of small, localized, mechanical maximizations taken together, none of which can be considered in isolation as you perform the strike. Notice "perform" and not simply "do": there is a looseness and non-mechanical flow that must be present in order to maximize power.

While it is imperative to break down each element of staff mechanics, it is just as important to realize that mastery of any movement involves linking all elements on a single thread.

Conclusions

Lots of things to think about, but what's the bottom line? In the Gospels, it is said that those who can be trusted with little can be trusted with much. In Zen, it is said that even a single drop of water should be reckoned mindfully. The great sage Anonymous reminds us to waste not, want not. What do these wisdoms have in common?

Attention to detail.

If you pay attention to the mechanics of your staff technique, your technique will improve. Shooting video of your solo and partner training is very enlightening and will help you spot myriad places where your technique could be improved. An ounce of humility here leads to pounds, if not tons, of improvement when you take those clips with you to your next practice.

Practicing staff fighting will help you learn from the inside of the fight what works and what doesn't. Keep a journal, record successes and failures. What felt just right? What didn't? What do you want to try again next time, and what might you never try again after eating some oppositional kinetic energy?

With attention to the mechanics, your technique will improve. With improved technique, you can maximize your strategy. With improved strategy and technique, you can maximize your effectiveness in staff fighting.

Start with mechanics. Build a strong foundation of understanding that translates into practice. Then, as one of my earliest teachers used to say, "Go do that a thousand times, then come back." There is no substitute for practice!

About Chris Hall

Chris Hall began his formal martial training in 1991 at the original Satori Dojo of Cuong Nhu Oriental Martial Arts at Gettysburg College under Sensei Kay Etheridge and later Sensei Don Walz. After repeated maulings at their hands (and feet, and occasionally sticks) as well as those of Sensei Joe Varady, he earned his black belt in 1995 and his Shodan in 1997. In addition to training in Cuong Nhu, Chris has earned rank or certification in aikido, Filipino martial arts, and combatives, and he has trained widely in a variety of styles. He is an avid marksman and hunter, training in pistol, rifle, shotgun, and traditional recurve longbow.

Chris is also an educator with twenty years' experience, fifteen of which have also been spent in educational leadership. He currently serves as an academic dean of the Covenant School in Charlottesville, Virginia, has been elected an associate fellow in the Alcuin Fellowship of the Society for Classical Learning, and has presented and published on science pedagogy in the classical and liberal arts traditions. Chris has served as a PK–8 science department chair and teacher of conceptual physics, earth science, astronomy, STEM, tracking and wilderness survival, mathematics, and reading. He is an avid microfarmer, and lives off the beaten path in central Virginia with his wife and three sons.

Appendix II

Additional Skills and Drills

What? You want more? OK, I can't blame you . . . because working with the staff is fun, and there is still so much to learn. There were a lot of staff drills and skills that I decided not to include in the main body of this book. To include them all would have distracted from the main focus, which is staff *fighting*. While these other drills may be useful for developing sensitivity with the staff, I left them out because, in the end, I felt that they did little to directly aid in your basic understanding of combat. This does not mean that these drills would not make valuable additions to your training regime. In fact, I encourage you to play with the staff and develop a multitude of skill sets with the weapon. Continue to explore and experiment. If for no other reason, do it because it is *fun!*

Here is a partial list of additional skills, drills, and activities that you can use to spice up your staff training:

Stretch and exercise with the staff. Use the staff as a tool to help you gain flexibility and strength. Place the staff across your shoulders and do torso twists, side stretches, back arches, steam engines, and twisting toe touches.

Balance the staff on your hand, finger, foot, or chin. With the help of an assistant to get you started, you can even balance a staff on the end of another staff.

Dexterity Drill: Try to keep a balloon aloft with your staff. Too easy, you say? Try this drill with two, three, or even four balloons. You can do this activity solo or with a partner. Every time a balloon touches the ground, do push-ups or sit-ups with your staff.

Twirling: There are several methods for twirling the staff. They include the propeller twirl in front and to the sides, helicopter twirl overhead, windmill twirl (behind the back), four-count (Japanese) figure eights with arm circles (a technique commonly used when twirling the nunchaku), and six-count (Chinese) figure eights, to name but a few. Attach a two-foot length of ribbon to each end of your staff for a demonstration or fun staff workout. You could even use clear tape to attach light sticks to your staff and twirl in the dark. Twirl into focused strikes.

Passing behind the back: This can be done vertically and horizontally, stationary and moving. Pass directly into a strike or other technique. Work these passes into your twirling practice until they flow smoothly and seamlessly.

Horizontal pass behind the back (stationary): Start from a ready position, but later this should be incorporated smoothly into a twirling series.

Move the staff to your right side.

Momentarily release with your left hand as you pass the staff behind your back, re-grasping thumb to thumb.

Release with your right hand as you swing the staff back around to the front.

Re-grab with your right hand, ready to strike or continue twirling.

Vertical pass behind the back (spinning forward): Start from a ready position, but later this should be incorporated smoothly into a twirling series. Move the staff to your right side.

Momentarily release with your left hand as you pass the staff behind your back, re-grasping thumb to thumb behind you.

Release with your right hand as you continue to twirl the staff, stepping behind you with your left foot, spinning your body counterclockwise.

Re-grab in front of you with your right hand.

Finish with a downward vertical strike.

Picking up the staff with your foot: good for recovering your staff quickly while keeping your eyes on the opponent. There are several ways to do this, the easiest one being rolling to the instep and kicking up.

Foot pick-up: Keep your eyes on your opponent.

Place your foot on the staff.

Roll the staff back and onto your instep.

Pop it up and into your hands.

Grasp the staff firmly.

Land in a fighting stance.

Throwing the staff: Toss your staff up in the air and catch it. Add a strike immediately after each catch. Use a push-pass to play catch with a partner.

Foot pass: Combine the two moves above by tossing the staff with your foot. It looks very cool to disarm your opponent and then be able to kick his staff back to him without moving.

Flipping the staff: Grasp one end of the staff and hold it out at arm's length. With a flick of your wrist, toss the end you are holding up into the air. Catch the tip of the staff as it comes up from underneath, ending in the same position you started from, and repeat.

Start with a 180-degree half rotation, working up to a 360-degree full rotation, then a 540-degree turn and a half, and finally a 720-degree double flip.

Rolling with the staff: Practice executing forward rolls, side rolls (log rolls), and backward rolls with a staff in your hands. Roll directly into blocks and strikes. You can use a roll to pick up a staff on the ground, starting with the staff lying close to your feet, and working up to using a dive roll to pick up a staff lying several feet away.

A right shoulder roll with the staff.

Push-ups with the staff: There are a variety of different kinds of push-ups that you can do with your staff to strengthen your entire body. Perform push-ups with both palms down, both palms up, and with mixed grips. You can also perform them with wide grip (1), standard width (2), close grip (3), or parallel to your body (4). Try doing pommel push-ups on the butt of the staff, holding the staff vertically in front of you (5).

Back bridge: Put the tip of the staff on the ground behind you. Use it to support you as you walk your hands down the staff to the ground. Walk your hands back up to return to a standing position.

Sit-ups: As with push-ups, there are many ways to perform sit-ups with the staff. One method is to hold the staff over your head, with your shoulders and feet off the ground. Tuck your legs in and pass the staff under your feet, assuming a yoga "boat" posture. Reverse the series, tucking back through to your original position, then repeat.

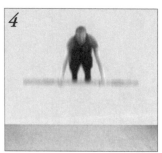

Jumping through the staff: If you get good at the sit-ups pictured above, you may be ready to try the tuck through while standing. Jump, passing the staff from front to back, then again passing from back to front.

Kicking with the staff. Try working in all your martial arts kicking techniques. Start with simple kicks, working up to spinning, jumping, and flying kicks.

Pole-vaulting with the staff: You can pole-vault over an obstacle. You can also use a pole vault in conjunction with a front instep kick to your open palm, a side kick, a cartwheel, or a "monkey lookout." Search *Chinese Monkey Staff Wu Shu* on YouTube for some inspiring performances, then start stealing techniques.

Staff juggling: Also known as contact staff, this is the art of manipulating the staff around your body. Experts perform with a fire staff. Again, I recommend searching YouTube for demonstrations and instruction.

Recommended Reading

Each of the following books lends a piece to the big puzzle. I encourage you to widen your knowledge and deepen your understanding through regular study.

Aoki, Hiroyuki. *Total Stick Fighting: Shintaido Bojutsu*. New York: Kodansha International, 2000.

Barbasetti, Luigi. *The Art of the Foil*. New York: E. P. Dutton & Co., Inc., 1932 (reprinted by Barnes & Noble Books, 1998).

Biddle, Lieut.-Col. A. J. Drexel, U.S.M.C.R., U.S.M.C. *Do or Die: A Supplementary Manual on Individual Combat*. 1937. Reprint, Boulder: Paladin Press, n.d.

Cheung, William. *Kung Fu Dragon Pole*. Valencia, CA: Black Belt Communications, 1989.

Demura, Fumio. *Bo: Karate weapon of Self-Defense*. Burbank, CA: Ohara Publications, 1976.

Leung, Ting. *The Ferocious Enchanted Staff of the Ancient Monks*. Hong Kong: Leung's Publications, 1986.

McLemore, Dwight C. *The Fighting Staff*. Boulder: Paladin Press, 2009.

Musashi, Miyamoto. *The Book of Five Rings*. New York: Overlook Press, 2001.

Preto, Luis, *Combat in Outnumbered Scenarios: The Origin of Historical Fencing*. Lexington, KY: CreateSpace Independent Publishing Platform, 2011.

———. *Fencing Martial Arts: How to Sequence the Teaching of Technique and Tactics*. Lexington, KY: CreateSpace Independent Publishing Platform, 2011.

———. *Staff, Baton, and Longsword Combat Series: Functional Parrying Skill*. Lexington, KY: CreateSpace Independent Publishing Platform, 2011.

———. *Staff, Baton, and Longsword Combat Series: Understanding and Developing Footwork*. Lexington, KY: CreateSpace Independent Publishing Platform, 2011.

Suino, Nicklaus. *Strategy in Japanese Swordsmanship*. Boston: Shambhala Publications, 2017.

Thompson, Lynn C. "King of Weapons." *Cold Steel*, 2000. www.coldsteel.com/files/Riposte/The-Spear.pdf.

You can also try looking up these keywords on search engines and YouTube: bo, kumibo, bojitsu, quarterstaff, staff fighting, jogo do pau, jojitsu, Dog Brothers, Donga stick fighting, cane fighting, Okinawan kobudo, padded weapons fighting, bongtoogi, chanbara, extreme martial arts, contact staff, staff juggling.

Absorb what is useful. Discard what is not.
Add what is uniquely your own.
—Bruce Lee

About the Author

Joe Varady, M.Ed.

Master Joe Varady has over thirty years' experience in the martial arts. He began Cuong Nhu Oriental Martial Arts in 1987 and currently holds a sixth-degree black belt. Over the past three decades, he has cross-trained in Eastern martial arts including karate, taekwondo, judo, wing chun, and eskrima (to name a few), and various Western martial arts, such as boxing, fencing, long sword, sword and shield, and various methods of armored fighting.

To test his skills, Joe attended the 2014 Northeast WEKAF (World Eskrima Kali Arnis Federation) Nationals in New York City, where he qualified for a spot on the US team, competing at the World Championships in Hungary. It was there that he took second place in the world in full-contact staff fighting and fourth in full-contact double stick fighting. Not one to rest on his laurels, in March of 2015 Joe not only won first place in full-contact single stick fighting at the Doce Pares World Championships in New York City, but he also won the Northeast Taiji Fencing Championships held in Philadelphia's Chinatown. He wrapped up the year by winning the Taiji Fencing League's 2015 Grand Championship.

Joe currently shares his vast martial arts knowledge as the head instructor of two programs: traditional martial arts through Satori Dojo and progressive weapons systems through Modern Gladiatorial Arts, both located in Phoenixville, Pennsylvania. He is also the current president of the Universal Systems of Martial Arts Organization, an active fellowship that provides practitioners of different styles of martial arts with an open forum for sharing techniques and principles.

BOOKS FROM YMAA

6 HEALING MOVEMENTS
101 REFLECTIONS ON TAI CHI CHUAN
108 INSIGHTS INTO TAI CHI CHUAN
ADVANCING IN TAE KWON DO
ANALYSIS OF SHAOLIN CHIN NA 2ND ED
ANCIENT CHINESE WEAPONS
THE ART AND SCIENCE OF STAFF FIGHTING
ART OF HOJO UNDO
ARTHRITIS RELIEF, 3RD ED.
BACK PAIN RELIEF, 2ND ED.
BAGUAZHANG, 2ND ED.
CARDIO KICKBOXING ELITE
CHIN NA IN GROUND FIGHTING
CHINESE FAST WRESTLING
CHINESE FITNESS
CHINESE TUI NA MASSAGE
CHOJUN
COMPREHENSIVE APPLICATIONS OF SHAOLIN
    CHIN NA
CONFLICT COMMUNICATION
CROCODILE AND THE CRANE: A NOVEL
CUTTING SEASON: A XENON PEARL MARTIAL ARTS THRILLER
DEFENSIVE TACTICS
DESHI: A CONNOR BURKE MARTIAL ARTS THRILLER
DIRTY GROUND
DR. WU'S HEAD MASSAGE
DUKKHA HUNGRY GHOSTS
DUKKHA REVERB
DUKKHA, THE SUFFERING: AN EYE FOR AN EYE
DUKKHA UNLOADED
ENZAN: THE FAR MOUNTAIN, A CONNOR BURKE MARTIAL ARTS
    THRILLER
ESSENCE OF SHAOLIN WHITE CRANE
EXPLORING TAI CHI
FACING VIOLENCE
FIGHT BACK
FIGHT LIKE A PHYSICIST
THE FIGHTER'S BODY
FIGHTER'S FACT BOOK
FIGHTER'S FACT BOOK 2
FIGHTING THE PAIN RESISTANT ATTACKER
FIRST DEFENSE
FORCE DECISIONS: A CITIZENS GUIDE
FOX BORROWS THE TIGER'S AWE
INSIDE TAI CHI
KAGE: THE SHADOW, A CONNOR BURKE MARTIAL ARTS
    THRILLER
KATA AND THE TRANSMISSION OF KNOWLEDGE
KRAV MAGA PROFESSIONAL TACTICS
KRAV MAGA WEAPON DEFENSES
LITTLE BLACK BOOK OF VIOLENCE
LIUHEBAFA FIVE CHARACTER SECRETS
MARTIAL ARTS ATHLETE
MARTIAL ARTS INSTRUCTION
MARTIAL WAY AND ITS VIRTUES
MASK OF THE KING
MEDITATIONS ON VIOLENCE
MERIDIAN QIGONG
MIND/BODY FITNESS
THE MIND INSIDE TAI CHI
THE MIND INSIDE YANG STYLE TAI CHI CHUAN
MUGAI RYU
NATURAL HEALING WITH QIGONG
NORTHERN SHAOLIN SWORD, 2ND ED.
OKINAWA'S COMPLETE KARATE SYSTEM: ISSHIN RYU
POWER BODY

PRINCIPLES OF TRADITIONAL CHINESE MEDICINE
QIGONG FOR HEALTH & MARTIAL ARTS 2ND ED.
QIGONG FOR LIVING
QIGONG FOR TREATING COMMON AILMENTS
QIGONG MASSAGE
QIGONG MEDITATION: EMBRYONIC BREATHING
QIGONG MEDITATION: SMALL CIRCULATION
QIGONG, THE SECRET OF YOUTH: DA MO'S CLASSICS
QUIET TEACHER: A XENON PEARL MARTIAL ARTS THRILLER
RAVEN'S WARRIOR
REDEMPTION
ROOT OF CHINESE QIGONG, 2ND ED.
SCALING FORCE
SENSEI: A CONNOR BURKE MARTIAL ARTS THRILLER
SHIHAN TE: THE BUNKAI OF KATA
SHIN GI TAI: KARATE TRAINING FOR BODY, MIND, AND SPIRIT
SIMPLE CHINESE MEDICINE
SIMPLE QIGONG EXERCISES FOR HEALTH, 3RD ED.
SIMPLIFIED TAI CHI CHUAN, 2ND ED.
SIMPLIFIED TAI CHI FOR BEGINNERS
SOLO TRAINING
SOLO TRAINING 2
SUDDEN DAWN: THE EPIC JOURNEY OF BODHIDHARMA
SUMO FOR MIXED MARTIAL ARTS
SUNRISE TAI CHI
SUNSET TAI CHI
SURVIVING ARMED ASSAULTS
TAE KWON DO: THE KOREAN MARTIAL ART
TAEKWONDO BLACK BELT POOMSAE
TAEKWONDO: A PATH TO EXCELLENCE
TAEKWONDO: ANCIENT WISDOM FOR THE MODERN WARRIOR
TAEKWONDO: DEFENSES AGAINST WEAPONS
TAEKWONDO: SPIRIT AND PRACTICE
TAO OF BIOENERGETICS
TAI CHI BALL QIGONG: FOR HEALTH AND MARTIAL ARTS
TAI CHI BALL WORKOUT FOR BEGINNERS
TAI CHI BOOK
TAI CHI CHIN NA: THE SEIZING ART OF TAI CHI CHUAN, 2ND ED.
TAI CHI CHUAN CLASSICAL YANG STYLE, 2ND ED.
TAI CHI CHUAN MARTIAL APPLICATIONS
TAI CHI CHUAN MARTIAL POWER, 3RD ED.
TAI CHI CONNECTIONS
TAI CHI DYNAMICS
TAI CHI QIGONG, 3RD ED.
TAI CHI SECRETS OF THE ANCIENT MASTERS
TAI CHI SECRETS OF THE WU & LI STYLES
TAI CHI SECRETS OF THE WU STYLE
TAI CHI SECRETS OF THE YANG STYLE
TAI CHI SWORD: CLASSICAL YANG STYLE, 2ND ED.
TAI CHI SWORD FOR BEGINNERS
TAI CHI WALKING
TAIJIQUAN THEORY OF DR. YANG, JWING-MING
TENGU: THE MOUNTAIN GOBLIN, A CONNOR BURKE MARTIAL
    ARTS THRILLER
TIMING IN THE FIGHTING ARTS
TRADITIONAL CHINESE HEALTH SECRETS
TRADITIONAL TAEKWONDO
TRAINING FOR SUDDEN VIOLENCE
WAY OF KATA
WAY OF KENDO AND KENJITSU
WAY OF SANCHIN KATA
WAY TO BLACK BELT
WESTERN HERBS FOR MARTIAL ARTISTS
WILD GOOSE QIGONG
WOMAN'S QIGONG GUIDE
XINGYIQUAN

DVDS FROM YMAA

ADVANCED PRACTICAL CHIN NA IN-DEPTH

ANALYSIS OF SHAOLIN CHIN NA

ATTACK THE ATTACK

BAGUAZHANG: EMEI BAGUAZHANG

CHEN STYLE TAIJIQUAN

CHIN NA IN-DEPTH COURSES 1—4

CHIN NA IN-DEPTH COURSES 5—8

CHIN NA IN-DEPTH COURSES 9—12

FACING VIOLENCE: 7 THINGS A MARTIAL ARTIST MUST KNOW

FIVE ANIMAL SPORTS

JOINT LOCKS

KNIFE DEFENSE: TRADITIONAL TECHNIQUES AGAINST A
   DAGGER

KUNG FU BODY CONDITIONING 1

KUNG FU BODY CONDITIONING 2

KUNG FU FOR KIDS

KUNG FU FOR TEENS

INFIGHTING

LOGIC OF VIOLENCE

MERIDIAN QIGONG

NEIGONG FOR MARTIAL ARTS

NORTHERN SHAOLIN SWORD : SAN CAI JIAN, KUN WU JIAN, QI MEN
   JIAN

QIGONG MASSAGE

QIGONG FOR HEALING

QIGONG FOR LONGEVITY

QIGONG FOR WOMEN

SABER FUNDAMENTAL TRAINING

SAI TRAINING AND SEQUENCES

SANCHIN KATA: TRADITIONAL TRAINING FOR KARATE POWER

SHAOLIN KUNG FU FUNDAMENTAL TRAINING: COURSES 1 & 2

SHAOLIN LONG FIST KUNG FU: BASIC SEQUENCES

SHAOLIN LONG FIST KUNG FU: INTERMEDIATE SEQUENCES

SHAOLIN LONG FIST KUNG FU: ADVANCED SEQUENCES 1

SHAOLIN LONG FIST KUNG FU: ADVANCED SEQUENCES 2

SHAOLIN SABER: BASIC SEQUENCES

SHAOLIN STAFF: BASIC SEQUENCES

SHAOLIN WHITE CRANE GONG FU BASIC TRAINING: COURSES 1 & 2

SHAOLIN WHITE CRANE GONG FU BASIC TRAINING: COURSES 3 & 4

SHUAI JIAO: KUNG FU WRESTLING

SIMPLE QIGONG EXERCISES FOR ARTHRITIS RELIEF

SIMPLE QIGONG EXERCISES FOR BACK PAIN RELIEF

SIMPLIFIED TAI CHI CHUAN: 24 & 48 POSTURES

SIMPLIFIED TAI CHI FOR BEGINNERS 48

SUNRISE TAI CHI

SUNSET TAI CHI

SWORD: FUNDAMENTAL TRAINING

TAEKWONDO KORYO POOMSAE

TAI CHI BALL QIGONG: COURSES 1 & 2

TAI CHI BALL QIGONG: COURSES 3 & 4

TAI CHI BALL WORKOUT FOR BEGINNERS

TAI CHI CHUAN CLASSICAL YANG STYLE

TAI CHI CONNECTIONS

TAI CHI ENERGY PATTERNS

TAI CHI FIGHTING SET

TAI CHI FIT FLOW

TAI CHI FIT STRENGTH

TAI CHI FOR WOMEN

TAI CHI PUSHING HANDS: COURSES 1 & 2

TAI CHI PUSHING HANDS: COURSES 3 & 4

TAI CHI SWORD: CLASSICAL YANG STYLE

TAI CHI SWORD FOR BEGINNERS

TAI CHI SYMBOL: YIN YANG STICKING HANDS

TAIJI & SHAOLIN STAFF: FUNDAMENTAL TRAINING

TAIJI CHIN NA IN-DEPTH

TAIJI 37 POSTURES MARTIAL APPLICATIONS

TAIJI SABER CLASSICAL YANG STYLE

TAIJI WRESTLING

TRAINING FOR SUDDEN VIOLENCE

UNDERSTANDING QIGONG 1: WHAT IS QI? • HUMAN QI
   CIRCULATORY SYSTEM

UNDERSTANDING QIGONG 2: KEY POINTS • QIGONG
   BREATHING

UNDERSTANDING QIGONG 3: EMBRYONIC BREATHING

UNDERSTANDING QIGONG 4: FOUR SEASONS QIGONG

UNDERSTANDING QIGONG 5: SMALL CIRCULATION

UNDERSTANDING QIGONG 6: MARTIAL QIGONG
   BREATHING

WHITE CRANE HARD & SOFT QIGONG

WUDANG KUNG FU: FUNDAMENTAL TRAINING

WUDANG SWORD

WUDANG TAIJIQUAN

XINGYIQUAN

YANG TAI CHI FOR BEGINNERS

YMAA 25 YEAR ANNIVERSARY DVD

more products available from . . .
YMAA Publication Center, Inc. 楊氏東方文化出版中心

1-800-669-8892 • info@ymaa.com • www.ymaa.com